Contents

KT-466-491

Why do historians differ?

THE purpose of the Flagship Historymakers series is to explore the main debates surrounding a number of key individuals in British, European and American History.

Each book begins with a chronology of the significant events in the life of the individual, and an outline of their career. The book then examines in greater detail three of the most important and controversial issues in the life of the individual – issues which continue to attract differing views from historians, and which feature prominently in examination syllabuses in A-level History and beyond.

Each of these sections provides students with an overview of the main arguments put forward by historians. By posing key questions these sections aim to help students to think through the areas of debate and to form their own judgements on the evidence. It is important, therefore, for students to understand why historians differ in their views on past events and, in particular, on the role of individuals in past events.

The study of history is an ongoing debate about events in the past. Although factual evidence is the essential ingredient of history it is the *interpretation* of factual evidence that forms the basis for historical debate. The study of how and why historians differ in their various interpretations is termed 'historiography'.

Historical debate can occur for a wide variety of reasons.

Insufficient evidence

In some cases there is insufficient evidence to provide a definitive conclusion. In attempting to 'fill the gaps' where factual evidence is unavailable, historians use their professional judgement to make 'informed comments' about the past.

Availability of evidence

An important reason why historical dabates occur is the availability of evidence on which to base historical judgements. As new evidence comes to light, an historian today may have more information on which to base judgements than historians in the past. For instance, major source of information about Nazi Germany are the diaries and reminiscences of Nazi leaders. The diaries of Josef Goebbels were published, in English, in the 1980s. Therefore, it is only relatively recently that historians have been able to analyse and assess this evidence.

A 'philosophy' of history?

Many historians have a specific view of history that will affect the way they make their historical judgements. For instance, Marxist historians – who take their view from the writings of Karl Marx, the founder of modern socialism – believe that society has been made up of competing economic and social classes. They also place considerable importance on economic reasons in human decision making. Therefore, a Marxist historian would regard Nazism as an extreme form of anti-communism. It would be regarded as an anti-modern, anti-progressive movement. This would be a completely different viewpoint to a non-Marxist historian.

The role of the individual

Some historians have seen history as being moulded by the acts of specific individuals. Hitler, Mussolini and Stalin would be seen as individuals who completely changed the course of 20th-century European history. Other historians have tended to 'downplay' the role of individuals; instead, they highlight the importance of more general social, economic and political change. Rather than seeing Adolf Hitler as an individual who changed the course of political history, these historians tend to see him as representing the views of a broader group of individuals: conservative, nationalist, anti-Semitic and anti-communist forces in inter-war Germany. Had Hitler not existed, another leader – perhaps Gregor Strasser or Goering – would have taken his place.

Placing different emphasis on the same historical evidence

Even if historians do not possess different philosophies of history or place different emphasis on the role of the individual, it is still possible for them to disagree in one very important way. This is that they may place different emphasis on aspects of the same factual evidence. As a result, History should be seen as a subject that encourages debate about the past, based on historical evidence.

Historians will always differ

Historical debate is, in its nature, continuous. What today may be an accepted view about a past event may well change in the future, as the debate continues.

Timeline: Hitler's life

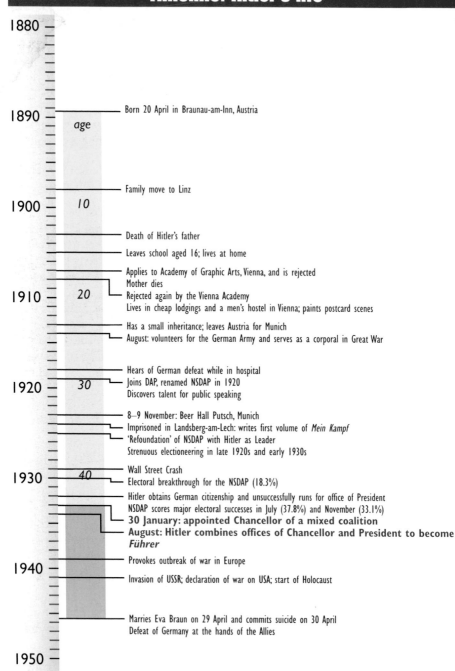

	age	
1880		
1890		Born 20 April in Braunau-am-Inn, Austria
1900	10	Family move to Linz
		Death of Hitler's father
		Leaves school aged 16; lives at home
		Applies to Academy of Graphic Arts, Vienna, and is rejected
		Mother dies
1910	20	Rejected again by the Vienna Academy
		Lives in cheap lodgings and a men's hostel in Vienna; paints postcard scenes
		Has a small inheritance; leaves Austria for Munich
		August: volunteers for the German Army and serves as a corporal in Great War
		Hears of German defeat while in hospital
1920	30	Joins DAP, renamed NSDAP in 1920
		Discovers talent for public speaking
		8–9 November: Beer Hall Putsch, Munich
		Imprisoned in Landsberg-am-Lech: writes first volume of *Mein Kampf*
		'Refoundation' of NSDAP with Hitler as Leader
		Strenuous electioneering in late 1920s and early 1930s
1930	40	Wall Street Crash
		Electoral breakthrough for the NSDAP (18.3%)
		Hitler obtains German citizenship and unsuccessfully runs for office of President
		NSDAP scores major electoral successes in July (37.8%) and November (33.1%)
		30 January: appointed Chancellor of a mixed coalition
		August: Hitler combines offices of Chancellor and President to become *Führer*
1940		Provokes outbreak of war in Europe
		Invasion of USSR; declaration of war on USA; start of Holocaust
		Marries Eva Braun on 29 April and commits suicide on 30 April
		Defeat of Germany at the hands of the Allies
1950		

itler in Nazi Party uniform, 1933.

Hitler: a brief biography

How did he make history?

Hitler is one of the most notorious individuals in modern history. Without Hitler, the Holocaust – the organised mass murder of around six million people on grounds of alleged 'racial inferiority' – would not have taken place. Nor, possibly, might the Second World War, which caused the deaths of around 55 million people, and brought unspeakable misery to millions more. The long-term consequences of Hitler's rule were enormous. Military defeat of Germany at the hands of the two new super-powers, the USA and the USSR, brought about the division of Europe in a new Cold War which dominated world affairs for the latter half of the 20th century. The importance of Hitler for understanding 20th-century European and world history cannot be over-estimated.

Or can it? Some historians would argue that Hitler's own personality, his oratorical powers and alleged 'charisma', have been grossly overstated. Was this nondescript upstart, this lower-middle class Austrian and failed art student, really just the beneficiary of wider forces sweeping Europe in the first half of the 20th century? Were not the economic and political crises in the 'age of extremes' really to blame for the rise of dictators of both left and right – Mussolini in Italy, Stalin in the Soviet Union, as well as Hitler in Germany? And was there not much in Germany's own longer-term history – peculiarities in culture, in 'belated' unification, in rapid and lop-sided political and economic modernisation – which might be just as important in explaining the **Third Reich**? Once in power, was Hitler really the 'strong dictator' depicted in propaganda? And after the collapse of Nazism, has too much blame been directed at Hitler himself, conveniently (for his many contemporaries) over-looking the roles of wider groups in German society? Controversies over the role of Hitler continue to rage furiously.

Third Reich: The 'Third Empire' (1933–45), following the (medieval and early modern) Holy Roman Empire of the German Nation and the (second) German Empire of 1871–1918.

Hitler's early years

Adolf Hitler was born the son of a minor Austrian customs official in the border town of Braunau-am-Inn on 20 April 1889. Although there has been speculation about possible Jewish ancestry, it is most likely that the murky illegitimate roots of Adolf Hitler's father – who was originally baptised Alois Schicklgruber and changed his surname in 1876 – concealed little more than some minor family scandal, possibly involving a degree of incest. Adolf Hitler was the fourth of six children of Alois' marriage to Klara Pölzl. Only one sister, Paula (1896–1960), survived to adulthood; there was also a half-sister and half-brother from one of his father's previous two marriages.

Hitler appears to have had a relatively happy childhood. But, after the family moved to Linz, Hitler's home life was increasingly overshadowed by rows with his overbearing father, for which his mother tried to compensate by showering Hitler with affection. Hitler's father died suddenly in January 1903, when Hitler was 13. As a teenager, Hitler had difficulty making relationships, and performed badly at his secondary school; he was eventually forced to leave and move to another school in Steyr, living in lodgings fifty miles from home. In 1905, at the age of 16, Hitler left school with neither qualifications nor clear plans for the future.

Drifter without aim

In the following years, Hitler drifted, idling for a couple of years at home, nurturing grand plans for a future in art and architecture. Then, at the age of 18 in 1907 he applied unsuccessfully to the Academy of Graphic Arts in Vienna. He suffered a further shattering blow with his mother's death from breast cancer at the age of 47 in December 1907. She seems to have been the one person with whom Hitler was able to form a genuinely close emotional bond. Following renewed failure to enter the Academy in 1908, Hitler lived the life of a respectable down-and-out, indulging his enthusiasm for the opera (particularly Wagner), and living austerely in cheap lodgings and, for a while, in a men's hostel. His position improved with financial help from his aunt, and additional modest earnings painting post-cards of Vienna.

During his time in Vienna, Hitler was influenced by widely prevalent anti-Semitic and nationalist ideas, and railed against the cosmopolitan character of the **Habsburg Empire**. He greatly admired Vienna's anti-Semitic mayor, Karl Lueger; but Hitler's own political 'activities' were limited to holding forth to a captive audience in the men's hostel. Hitler also had a couple of Jewish associates who helped him sell his pictures; and indeed, his mother's own doctor, whom Hitler thanked for tending her in her last illness, had been Jewish.

In 1913, aged 24, Hitler finally received his share of his father's inheritance. Having evaded military service in the hated Austrian army since 1909, Hitler took the opportunity to leave Austria for Munich. Tracked down by the Austrian authorities, after years of drifting, he was found unfit for military service. Yet in August 1914,

Habsburg Empire: the large multi-national empire of Austria-Hungary (since 1867), ruled by the Austrian Habsburg family. It included not only the German-speaking lands of Austria, but also Hungarians, Serbs, Croats, Slovaks, Romanians, Czechs, Slovenes, Italians and Poles.

when war was declared, in a fit of enthusiasm Hitler volunteer and was joined up – through bureaucratic oversight – in a Bavari regiment of the German army.

The making of a politician

The First World War and its aftermath proved the making of Hitl He enjoyed the camaraderie of the trenches and the role he held dispatch runner to the front; he received the Iron Cross twice f bravery, though he was not thought to show 'leadership potenti and was not promoted. His earlier prejudices took firmer shap when he heard of the end of hostilities in November 1918, while hospital recovering from a mustard gas attack, he was firm convinced that 'Jews' and **Bolsheviks** were to blame for a 'stab in t back' which caused Germany's defeat.

Bolsheviks: Originally the name for the Communist Party which led the Russian Revolution of October 1917, the term was generalised by the Nazis to apply not only to Communists but even to moderate socialists.

In 1919–20, Hitler remained as long as possible in Army emplo ment as a 'political education officer'. He discovered that possessed some talent for public speaking, and was able to stir t emotions of like-minded audiences. Having in the course of h army duties joined the German Workers' Party (DAP), a sm *völkisch* (right-wing nationalist) party led by Anton Drexler, Hitl rapidly emerged as a leading figure in the renamed Nation Socialist German Workers' Party (NSDAP).

Beer Hall Putsch: The Nazis' attempt, starting from Munich, to march on Berlin and take over the national government.

Following the NSDAP's abortive Munich **Beer Hall Putsch** November 1923 – one of many such uprisings at this turbule time – Hitler made a propaganda success of the trial. A sympathet judge pronounced a remarkably lenient sentence. In Landsbe prison, Hitler dictated the first volume of *Mein Kampf*, a ramblin and self-serving diatribe full of anti-Semitic prejudices. He w released early, in time for Christmas 1924.

Marxists: Technically, followers of the revolutionary ideas of Karl Marx, but the term was greatly over-generalised by the Nazis.

Social Democrats: Moderate socialists committed to reform by democratic means.

The rise to power

In Hitler's absence, the Nazi movement had splintered. C returning to active politics in 1925 with the 'refoundation' of t NSDAP, Hitler alone proved able to unite the different factions of t party. Now the 'leadership principle' emerged: Hitler himself, Leader, now embodied the Nazi Movement; there were to be n further debates about the party's Programme.

Social Darwinism: The application of Charles Darwin's evolutionary theories, including the notion of 'natural selection' and the 'survival of the fittest', to society.

The key points of Hitler's world view were by now clear: hatred Jews and **Marxists**, including **Social Democrats**; racial ideology an **Social Darwinism**; critique of the evils of modern capitalism, fro big department stores and international finance to cultur **decadence** (all allegedly 'Jewish'); demands for revision of the har

Cultural decadence: A sense that aspects of modern culture were characterised by immorality and the decay of traditional values.

Understanding Hitler

- The son of a minor Austrian customs official, Hitler seemed to speak for the 'little man' and the masses.

- Ill-educated and not an original thinker, Hitler acquired enough 'knowledge' to bolster his prejudices.

- Hitler was fascinated by the visual enactment of power, from the vague art plans of his boyhood, through the political ceremonies, parades and propaganda of the Nazi state, to grandiose architectural dreams for the future face of the Thousand-year Reich.

- Awkward in smaller circles, Hitler was a gifted speaker in large, well-organised settings with a receptive audience.

- Hitler's alleged 'charisma' was as much a matter of the economic and political circumstances as it was of his own personal attributes.

- Hitler was more concerned with his long-term racial and foreign policy goals than with the day-to-day details of policy.

- Hitler's work habits were highly disorganised. He tended to get up late and had little interest in paperwork or the organised practices of 'normal' bureaucratic government.

- Hitler preferred to set the tone and the ultimate goals, and let his subordinates 'fight it out' among themselves.

- Essentially a moody person, Hitler was also given to using controlled outbursts of temper to achieve what he wanted.

- Hitler was an opportunist who turned circumstances to his own advantage; he was also very often simply lucky.

- Hitler, a teetotaller who first became a vegetarian for health reasons in 1924, cultivated an image of kindness to children and animals.

- Hitler was totally without moral scruples, using violence and murder whenever it suited him.

'Hitler is ... the purest embodiment of a National Socialist Germany'
Nazi supporter
'Nothing more than a lance-corporal: a conceited braggart'
Fränkische Tagespost, 24 October 1932

1919 Treaty of Versailles, and for territorial expansion to acquire mor
Lebensraum ('living space') for Germans.

As the Depression deepened after the Wall Street Crash of 192!
Hitler's message began to spread. The apparent youth an
dynamism of the Nazi movement, with its claims to be a 'party o
the people', attracted many voters in a time of crisis. The NSDA
achieved its first electoral breakthrough in 1930; and in 1932, a yea
of acute political instability, it became the largest party in th
Reichstag (German parliament), though its fortunes declined in th
autumn. It was in the same year that Hitler (unsuccessfully seekin
election as President) finally acquired German citizenship. But
was due to a complex combination of factors that, at the age of 43 i
January 1933, Adolf Hitler, despised as the upstart 'Bohemia
corporal', was constitutionally appointed Chancellor of Germany b
the ageing President Paul von Hindenburg.

Hitler as *Führer*

Once in office, Hitler rapidly destroyed what remained of Weima
democracy. With the death of President Hindenburg in 1934, Hitl
combined the offices of Chancellor and President to becom

Führer: literally, 'leader'.
Hitler's self-designation,
combining the
constitutional roles of
President and Chancellor
into a new and ill-defined
supreme role as
charismatic saviour and
representative of the
German people.

absolute *Führer* (or charismatic 'Leader'), thus combining form.
ceremonial and political power with a demagogic appeal to th
masses.

Hitler's obsessions were put into immediate effect, with discrim
ination against Jews and the 'hereditarily diseased' and brut.
persecution of political opponents. In the mid-1930s, the return t
full employment, a degree of consumer satisfaction, and certai
peaceful foreign policy successes brought considerable popul.
support for Hitler, who also fostered his image as charismat
Führer. But Hitler's power was inherently unstable.

Blitzkrieg: 'Lightning
war' with spectacularly
quick military successes.

Even in the first two years of the war, with military success
across Europe in the *Blitzkrieg*, Hitler retained some popularity.
was only in 1941, with the invasion of the USSR and declaration o
war on the USA, that the tide began to turn. Hitler's dual goals o
racial 'cleansing', culminating in mass genocide, and milita
'world mastery', culminating in world war, were ultimately to prov
fatal for Hitler himself as well as for the millions whose deaths h
had caused.

Hitler had little by way of a private life outside politics. He ha
been a loner in Vienna and even among comrades in the trenches
the Great War, although he developed intense relationships wit
close political associates later on. A brief entanglement with h

va Braun (1910–45):
tler's long-term female
mpanion.

half-niece, Angela ('Geli') Raubel, ended in her suicide at the age of 23 in 1931; subsequently Hitler developed a liaison with **Eva Braun**. Always a hypochondriac, Hitler increasingly took medications which exacerbated his stormy moods, causing him to withdraw ever more from public life. As his dream of a 'Thousand-year Reich' lay shattered and Russian troops moved into the ruins of Berlin, Hitler despaired. On 29 April 1945, in his underground bunker, Hitler married Eva Braun; on 30 April, alongside Eva Braun, at the age of 56 Adolf Hitler committed suicide.

er's Bavarian mountain retreat, the Berghof on the Obersalzburg near Berchtesgaden.

1 Why was there so little internal opposition?

How important were propaganda and indoctrination in producing consent?

What was the role of terror and coercion?

Who opposed Hitler and why were they not more successful?

Framework of events

1933	Hitler appointed Chancellor
	Goebbels becomes head of new Reich Ministry for Propaganda and Popular Enlightenme
	Dachau concentration camp established
	Burning of books written by 'undesirable' authors
	'Law against the Establishment of Political Parties': one-party state
1934	'Night of the Long Knives'
	SS under Himmler becomes independent of SA
	Death of President Hindenburg. Army swears allegiance to Hitler
1936	Sachsenhausen concentration camp established
1937	Buchenwald concentration camp established
1938	Flossenbürg and Mauthausen concentration camps established
	Unsuccessful attempts by Ludwig Beck and conspirators to topple Hitler
1939	German invasion of Poland
	Britain and France declare war on Germany
	RSHA as headquarters of repression, uniting the Gestapo, the criminal police, the SD and the SS
	Elser's attempt to assassinate Hitler in Munich
1941	Bishop von Galen protests against euthanasia programme
1942	'Red Orchestra' group crushed by Gestapo
	Construction of concentration camps designed for extermination, including: Auschwitz II a Birkenau, Sobibor, Treblinka, Belzec and Maidenek
1943	Goebbels' 'total war' speech at Berlin Sports Palace
	'White Rose' resistance group destroyed
1944	'July Plot' crushed

HITLER was not brought to power in January 1933 on a tidal wave of popular support; nor did he 'seize power'. Rather, in the context of political stalemate and constitutional crisis, Hitler was appointed Chancellor in a mixed cabinet, by the ageing President Hindenburg. Prior to 1933, the Nazi vote had been volatile: climbing within five years from a mere 2.6 per cent in 1928 to more than one in three of the voters (37.8 per cent) at the height of economic depression and political crisis in July 1932. It then declined again to 33.1 per cent in November 1932. In January 1933, Hitler was still leader of the largest party; but even in the General Election of March 1933, the **NSDAP** failed to score more than 44 per cent of the vote.

In the following twelve years, Hitler's popularity first soared, with economic recovery and foreign policy successes, and then, with a reversal of Germany's fortunes in war, declined. Throughout the period, too, an increasingly formidable apparatus of repression and terror accompanied Nazi attempts to produce ideological conformity, and while a minority of Germans opposed Hitler in a variety of ways, none were ultimately successful.

NSDAP:
ationalsozialistische eutsche Arbeiterpartei National Socialist German orkers' Party).

How important were propaganda and indoctrination in producing consent?

There are difficulties with ascertaining levels of popular support in a dictatorship. While the results of rigged elections and direct votes by the controlling party in a one-party state can indicate high levels of support at certain times (as Robert Gellately argues in *Backing Hitler*), such results nevertheless have to be treated with a considerable degree of scepticism. While the regime's own reports from the security service or ***Sicherheitsdienst (SD)*** tended pessimistically to underestimate popular support, the reports of the Social Democratic Party in exile (SOPADE) tended, equally pessimistically but from the opposite perspective, to overestimate support. Historians have also used other types of evidence – diaries, letters, even the wording used in newspaper death notices (as in Ian Kershaw's *The Hitler Myth*) – to gauge popular opinion. Widespread voluntary cooperation in the implementation of policies and in the *Gleichschaltung* ('co-ordination') of organisations is also indicative of general agreement.

icherheitsdienst, **D** ('Security Service'): the :elligence branch of the under Reinhard ydrich

Ian Kershaw, *The 'Hitler Myth': Image and Reality in the Third Reich*
(Oxford University Press, 1987), and
Popular Opinion and Political Dissent in the Third Reich
(Oxford: Clarendon Press, 1983)

These two books — which initially arose from the same research project on Bavaria, and explore two sides of the same coin — have contributed significantly to the development of more sophisticated interpretations of popular opinion in the Third Reich. Exploring the ambiguities, inconsistencies and variations in patterns of attitudes and behaviour among ordinary people, Kershaw shows that simple contrasts between 'support' and 'opposition', 'consent' and 'coercion', 'indoctrination' and 'repression', do not adequately fit all the evidence. Kershaw's research demonstrates the importance of the myth of the *Führer* as a saviour figure, an element of cohesion in an increasingly chaotic political system: thus people could have great faith in Hitler while at the same time criticising many aspects of everyday life. And widespread apathy might be just as important as active support in allowing the regime to pursue policies of the utmost inhumanity.

Overt propaganda

**Josef Goebbels
(1897–1945)**
Joseph Goebbels poured his intellectual energy into propaganda for the Nazi party. He joined in 1926 and took over the Berlin section of the NSDAP. In 1929 he became 'Reich Propaganda Leader', and was instrumental in the NSDAP's subsequent election successes. In March 1933 Goebbels became 'Reich Minister for Public Enlightenment and Propaganda', with total control over the press, radio and film. He played a key role in anti-Semitic events. He stayed with Hitler in the bunker to the last, and then, after poisoning his children, committed suicide alongside his wife, Magda.

Control and manipulation of the news was of considerabl importance. **Josef Goebbels**, appointed Minister of Propagand and Public Enlightenment in March 1933, rapidly sought t bring the highly diverse regional press of Germany unde increasing Nazi control, through central control of editors an journalists under Max Amann's Reich Press Chamber. The Naz newspaper, the *Völkische Beobachter*, increased in circulatio and more Germans felt they needed to pay attention to it. Radi ownership expanded rapidly: by the outbreak of war, betwee two-thirds and three-quarters of Germans had access to a radic Goebbels ensured not only that Nazi speeches and bombasti news bulletins were broadcast, but that there was no escap from exposure: radio broadcasts were boomed out in publi places – cafés, squares – to Germans who did not possess a radi in their own homes or who might not want to listen to suc bulletins.

Sophisticated visual representations were crucial. The arch tect Albert Speer was employed to design the buildings an townscapes of the 'master race', while 'German art' was celebrate and 'degenerate art' (by Jews, socialists and other 'undesirables was banned and denigrated. A talented young film-maker, Le Riefenstahl, produced two famous 'documentaries': *Triumph the Will* depicted Hitler in the context of the 1934 Nurember party rally, while *Olympia* deployed new cinematograph techniques to create powerful images of strength at the Berli Olympics of 1936. The German film industry went into th mass production of light entertainment films, which fa

out-numbered obvious propaganda films, seeking to build up a sense of well-being. But Goebbels also knew when it was important to strike terror into people's hearts. As the devastating effects of 'total war' became all too obvious, Goebbels – most notably in his speech of February 1943 at the Berlin Sports Palace – turned to a more 'realistic' depiction of the situation and the 'Bolshevik threat' in an attempt to goad Germans into making the ultimate sacrifice for their country.

Racism was a major theme. Overt attempts at anti-Semitic propaganda were evident in films such as *Jud Süss*, about an eighteenth-century court Jew in the Duchy of Württemberg, and even more so in *Der ewige Jude* ('The eternal Jew'), with accompanying posters, and in Julius Streicher's rabidly racist magazine *Der Stürmer*. In stark contrast, there were more 'positive' images of the *Volksgemeinschaft* ('people's community') with members of the '**Aryan**' or '**master race**' in posters advertising, for example, the benefits of the *Kraft durch Freude* ('Strength through Joy') programme, or the Nazi youth organisations (*HJ* and *BdM*). Even the theme of 'sacrifice' could be made the subject of a compelling poster, as in advertisements to participate in the *Eintopf* ('One Pot') meals in support of the national economic effort.

Thus propaganda was all around, and unavoidable. But two further elements appear to have been equally, if not more, important in producing consent.

The 'Hitler Myth' and the 'congruence of aims'

The first element is the 'Hitler myth'. As Ian Kershaw has brilliantly demonstrated, Hitler's role as charismatic *Führer* functioned as a major mechanism for cohesion. The *Führer* was projected as the saviour figure, above the fray, leading Germany onwards and upwards to a glorious future. If people were irritated by the squabbles and corruption of local NSDAP big-wigs, or annoyed by policies which adversely affected their own material interests, they could still take consolation in the belief that 'if only the *Führer* knew', all would be set to rights. The myth was carefully nurtured by Hitler, who stayed clear of day-to-day policy-making and spats between his subordinates, and instead paid close attention not merely to the contents of his speeches but also to body language and the ways in which power was 'enacted' in rallies and other public representations.

The second element is the question of the similarities between Nazi policies and the aims of different social groups, plus the way in which the government of the Third Reich actually succeeded in achieving widely shared aims. Popular support required more than propaganda, it was also dependent on improvements in the economic sphere and successes in foreign policy. Very few Germans shared Hitler's desire for war, although many were relieved and indeed elated by the rapid victories in the first two years of war. However, as the war progressed, the difference between ideology and reality became ever more apparent.

Defeat of the German army at Stalingrad dealt a death blow, not merely to the German military effort, but also to the Hitler myth. No amount of propaganda could disguise the truth. Hitler's personal popularity, and with it popular support for the regime, began to wane well before the final defeat.

What was the role of terror and coercion?

The Nazi system of terror was the other side of the coin. Popular conceptions of the Third Reich are filled not only with images of adoring admirers of the Führer, but also of the brutality of jack-booted SS officers and horror scenes of corpses in concentration camps. After 1945, fear of Nazi repression was a convenient excuse for many Germans. But the picture is more complex.

SA: the brown-shirted *Sturmabteilung* ('storm troopers'), a paramilitary organisation of the NSDAP.

The changing balance of forces of repression

Violence was an integral part of Hitler's rise to power: the brown-shirted **SA** (*'Sturmabteilung'*) was effectively a private army

Weimar Republic: the Republic created following the abdication of the Kaiser in November 1918, and named after the town of Weimar in which its first parliament met in 1919 as a result of the continuing political unrest in Berlin at the time.

beating up political opponents on the streets and contributing greatly to the chaos of the closing months of the **Weimar Republic** – a chaos which Hitler ironically promised to solve. The immediate 'solution' to political violence was simply to outlaw political opponents and to 'legalise' only the Nazi use of force. Within weeks of Hitler's appointment as Chancellor, a system of informal prisons and labour camps was set up, with political opponents – mainly communists and socialists – being rounded up and incarcerated. The first more permanent concentration camp was opened in March 1933, at Dachau, a small town just north-west of the Bavarian capital Munich. Its opening was accompanied by much publicity, and generally favourable public reactions.

There were a number of key shifts in the balance of forces of repression in the Third Reich. The first came in 1934. The SA, under the leadership of **Ernst Röhm**, had grown massively in size and aspirations, and presented a growing challenge. In the uncertain conditions of 1934, with top priority being given by Hitler to rearmament, it appeared essential to retain the backing of the professional Army. In the so-called '**Night of the Long Knives**' – actually stretching over three days at the end of June and beginning of July – Ernst Röhm and other SA leaders were assassinated, along with other individuals (numbering somewhere between 85 and 200) with whom Hitler wanted to settle old scores. The mass murder was retroactively sanctioned by a law in early July. When President Hindenburg died in August, the Army, now restored to what they saw as their rightful place, swore a personal oath of allegiance to Hitler. This military sense of honour and being bound by one's oath was later used to justify obedience to Hitler. Curiously, even conservatives with such a strong belief in 'honour' had managed to swallow their scruples and had failed to protest against the blatant resort to murder.

Night of the Long Knives: the murders on 30 June 1934 (continuing until 2 July) of senior members of the SA, including its leader Ernst Röhm, and other political targets. The total number murdered was somewhere between 85 and 200 people.

Ernst Röhm (1887–1934)

Röhm was an early member of the NSDAP, a close friend of Hitler, and a participant in the unsuccessful 1923 Beer Hall Putsch (which ended his career in the Army). Röhm built up the NSDAP's paramilitary wing, the SA (*Sturmabteilung* or Stormtroopers). The SA under his leadership became an ever larger and more radical force in German politics, greatly contributing to the political violence of the late Weimar years. By 1933–4, an increasingly powerful and independent SA posed a threat to the Army and to Hitler's strategies of 'legality' once in power. Röhm was thus the prime target of the 'Night of the Long Knives' in 1934. Röhm himself was arrested and shot in a prison cell after he refused to commit suicide.

**Heinrich Himmler
(1900–45)**

Himmler participated in the 1923 Beer Hall Putsch and was appointed head of the SS (*Schutzstaffel*) in January 1929. Himmler organised the purge of the SA and built up the SS, which became the key instrument of terror in the Nazi state. In 1936 Himmler became 'Reichsführer SS and Chief of the German Police in the Ministry of the Interior',

thus controlling both the regular police force and the security police. During the war, he controlled a veritable empire of power through the 'Reich Security Main Office' (RSHA), the criminal police and the Gestapo, as well as the various sections of the SS and Waffen-SS. He also oversaw and masterminded the 'Final Solution of the

Jewish Question'. On being arrested by the British at the end of the war, Himmler committed suicide with a poison pill.

SS *Schutzstaffel* ('protection squads'): the security force headed by Heinrich Himmler, which grew to be immensely powerful in the Third Reich, including responsibility for the operation of the concentration camps.

In the course of the 1930s, another new power rose rapidly prominence: the **SS ('*Schutzstaffel*')**. Originating as Hitler personal bodyguard, its leader from 1929 was **Heinrich Himmler**, a effective empire builder who had first joined the SS in 1925 when was but a small component of the SA. Under Himmler, the SS gre rapidly, and acquired a dedicated intelligence branch, the Securi Service or SD (*Sicherheitsdienst*) led by **Reinhard Heydrich**.

Himmler also soon began to gain control of the regular ar secret police forces, becoming police commander for Bavaria April 1933, and Inspector of the Gestapo (*Geheime Staatspolizei*, secret state police) in the powerful state of Prussia in April 193 Having played a key role in the Night of the Long Knives, in Ju 1934 Himmler secured the independence of the SS from the SA ar gained sole responsibility for running the concentration camps. 1936, Himmler officially added the control of the convention police forces across Germany to his empire, now boasting the tit of 'Reichsführer-SS and Chief of the German Police in the Reic Ministry of the Interior'. In 1939, alongside the SS, Himml coordinated the Gestapo, the SD, the criminal and the ordina

**Reinhard Heydrich
(1904–42)**

In July 1931, Heydrich joined the NSDAP and then the SS. Tall, blond and blue-eyed, he soon became Himmler's right-hand man, and from 1936 controlled the security police in the Reich. He became head of the RSHA in 1939, thus controlling the Gestapo, the criminal police and the SD. Heydrich played a major

role in the 'Final Solution of the Jewish Question', directing the *Einsatzgruppen* who carried out mass killings in the Soviet Union in 1941, and convening the 'Wannsee Conference' of January 1942 to coordinate the implementation of genocide. He became Deputy Reich Protector of Bohemia and Moravia in September

1941, and died on 4th June 1942 following an attack by two members of the Czech Resistance. His assassination was hideously avenged by complete destruction of the village of Lidice where it occurred and estimates of perhaps 1300 to 4000 related murders.

Heinrich Himmler with SS leaders, 1933.

RSHA
Reichssicherheits-hauptamt (Reich Security Head Office): umbrella organisation from 1939 designed to coordinate the work of the Gestapo, the SD, and the criminal and ordinary police forces alongside the SS.

Einsatzgruppen: extermination squads following the Army behind the lines and rounding up and murdering those who were ideologically designated targets of the Nazi regime (Jews, gypsies and other 'undesirables').

police forces under the umbrella of the **Reich Security Main Office (RSHA)**, headed by Heydrich. The internal organisation of the expanded SS was also increasingly specialised, with different units in charge of concentration camps, economic enterprises, educational and reproductive centres, as well as elite military units and *Einsatzgruppen* ('extermination squads').

Once the SS had taken control of the camp system, smaller, 'wild' camps were closed, and further camps were established. While Dachau had mainly held political prisoners, the new camps of the 1930s also took in 'asocials': not merely 'habitual criminals', but also people who simply refused to conform to Nazi societal norms, despite breaking none of the new laws. These people included Jehovah's Witnesses and homosexuals, as well as the allegedly 'work-shy' and people identified as gypsies, beggars and tramps, who could now be forced into slave labour. Ultimately, alongside these victims, the major targets of the extermination camps which were set up under the control of the SS from 1941 were Jews (see chapter three).

Ordinary Germans and the system of terror

Ordinary Germans were well aware of the brutal treatment received by opponents of the regime. Given the dread that this system of terror struck in the hearts of those opposed to the regime, it seems remarkable that many otherwise apolitical Germans actually welcomed the tough new line on 'criminals', the 'work-shy' and other 'asocials'. Also welcomed was the radical approach to Bolshevism, fear of which had played a large role in pre-1933 support for Hitler. Many initially felt that the wave of terror was essential to the restoration of stability. They believed that, despite the real growth in the apparatus of terror, by the mid-1930s a 'return to normality' was occurring.

Nazi terror, as Eric Johnson has shown in *The Nazi Terror. Gestapo, Jews and Ordinary Germans* (1999), was 'a selective terror' and it came in waves. Political and other opponents of the regime were among the first to be targeted and a variety of groups deemed in some way inferior or even 'unworthy of life' were to follow. A constant and vital target for the regime were the Jews. Those Germans who fell into none of these groups were largely able to ignore the repression. In *The Gestapo and German Society* (1990) Robert Gellately has shown how a relatively small Gestapo staff was even able to rely on voluntary denunciations by neighbours and colleagues. Overall, the German population was characterised by a degree of apathy.

Who opposed Hitler and why were they not more successful?

The question of dissent and opposition in Nazi Germany has been the subject not merely of historical but also political controversy. In East Germany, the allegedly leading role of communist resistance was celebrated, with some recognition being given to socialists, Christians and others who had fought alongside the communists. In West Germany, by contrast, the role of the conservative nationalist resistance to Hitler, and in particular the July Plot of 1944, was awarded great prominence. In the course of the 1960s, however, western historians began to explore a wider range of dissent, resistance and opposition, as traditional approaches to political history were increasingly challenged. Such challenges were complemented by new developments in social history and the history of everyday life, or 'history from below'. (See M. Fulbrook, *German National Identity after the Holocaust*, 1999.)

More recent debates are rooted partly in disagreements over definition. Attempts to assassinate Hitler clearly constitute opposition in a strong sense; this is often termed 'resistance' by

English-speaking historians. 'Dissent' may be disagreement with the regime, and 'non-conformity' is behaviour defined by the regime as unacceptable or illegal. But what of more mundane acts of 'refusal', such as refusal to give the 'Heil Hitler' salute, or to hang out a swastika flag? This is rather different from trying to overthrow the regime and its leader.

The German historian Martin Broszat widened debates over definition when he used the German word *'Resistenz'*, or 'resistance' in the medical sense of 'immunity to infection', as in the case of Catholics or certain young people who were simply impervious to the Nazi message. His approach provoked controversy over whether it is actual behaviour and its effects, or rather motives and intentions, that are crucial to the definition of resistance. These debates stimulated a wide range of research into areas such as the varieties of grumbling and disaffection in everyday life.

Dissent and nonconformity in everyday life

Much of the low-level grumbling that went on was in defence of personal material interests (see Ian Kershaw, *Popular Opinion and Political Dissent in the Third Reich*). Peasants grumbled about the Entailed Farm Law (which sought to tie peasants to ancestral land by ensuring that farms were not sub-divided but inherited whole) and tried to get around policies controlling the sale of agricultural produce. Workers sometimes engaged in unofficial strikes and go-slows; but there was a lack of consistent opposition among the German working class, despite the best efforts of Marxist historians such as Tim Mason to find it. The existence instead of a patchy record of partial compliance and non-compliance has been explored by Alf Lüdtke and others. Periodic grumbling was perfectly compatible with support for other developments, such as foreign policy successes, and enthusiasm for the *Führer*.

Other people engaged in more explicit acts of non-conformity (see Detlev Peukert, *Inside Nazi Germany*, 1987). In towns across Germany there were small groups of generally working class young people who refused to go along with the official Hitler Youth movement: the 'Edelweiss Pirates', the 'mobs' (*Meuten*) in Leipzig and Dresden, the *'Blasen'* (a slang word for 'mob') in Munich, and the 'Deathshead gang' and 'Bismarck gang' in Hamburg. Among middle class young people there were groups who insisted on listening to and playing jazz music. Many Germans of all ages refused to give up listening to or reading the works of 'Jewish' composers and authors, or enjoying 'decadent' art; and many continued to listen to foreign radio broadcast: make political jokes, or speak realistically – which was seen to b engaging in 'defeatism' – about the progress of the war.

These kinds of dissent were essentially demonstrative rathe than effective, allowing many Germans to hibernate through th regime in a state of 'inner emigration', and illustrating the Na: state's failure to achieve its total claims.

Organised groups and political parties

Gleichschaltung. Literally, 'putting into the same gear', or 'co-ordinating'; a term used to describe the ways in which organisations were 'brought into line' with Nazi aims and policies (or either forced to disband or outlawed).

Following the early period of **Gleichschaltung**, there were n independent institutional bases for organised opposition. Th Communist Party (KPD) was first to be outlawed, followed by th Social Democratic Party (SPD), whose leaders had spoken ou against the Enabling Act of 23 March. With the Concordat betwee Hitler and Pope, the Catholic Church received guarantee protecting religious practice, and the Catholic Centre Part dissolved itself. Similar fates befell the other political parties, and with the 'Law against the Formation of New Parties' of 14 Jul 1933, the Third Reich became a one-party state.

Thousands of left-wing opponents of the regime found they wer among its first targets, and were arrested and imprisoned in the earl wave of terror. In the new conditions of underground organisatio within the dictatorship, and following a change of line in Moscow i 1934, many left-wingers sought to transcend ideological hostilitie and work together against the common enemy, but conditions wer now far more difficult. Groups such as *Neubeginnen* ('Nev Beginning') met under extremely difficult circumstances, and wer able to achieve little by way of visible effects. At a higher level, th members of the 'Red Orchestra' group working within the goverr ment, including Harro Schulze-Boysen and Arvid Harnack, sougr to pass military intelligence to the Soviet Union, again with littl practical effect. There was very much less that ordinary worker could do, far as they were from the levers of power: sabotagin munitions production or circulating underground leaflets served t maintain some morale. But by no means did all workers have left wing sympathies, and denunciation and betrayal were no uncommon. It took only a few years of Nazi terror and torture t break the back of ordinary socialists and communists.

The Christian Churches

One might have thought that the institutional and moral power of th Christian Churches could have provided a strong base for principle

**Dietrich Bonhoeffer
(1906–45)**
A Protestant theologian and active participant in the 'Confessing Church' (*Bekennende Kirche*), Bonhoeffer put his spiritual and political energies into trying to assist all those who were persecuted by the Nazi regime. In 1939 in Britain, and again in 1942 in Sweden, Bonhoeffer sought unsuccessfully to act as an agent with foreign governments on behalf of high-placed conspirators against Hitler (including Beck and Oster). He was arrested by the Gestapo and imprisoned in 1943. Following the failure of the July Plot of 1944, Bonhoeffer was sent to Buchenwald concentration camp, and then to Flossenburg, where he was executed in April 1945. To this day, his theology has remained highly influential amongst Protestants, especially in Britain and the USA.

opposition. But such opposition was in fact patchy: a few key campaigns, a few outstanding and courageous individuals, stand out against a more ambivalent picture of compromise and conformity.

Hitler sought at first to 'co-ordinate' the Churches under the Nazi umbrella, or at least render them neutral. The attempt to incorporate Protestants in the Nazi fold, as pro-Nazi *Deutsche Christen* ('German Christians') under a Reich Bishop was unsuccessful. Those pastors who found themselves in trouble with the new regime soon formed the nucleus of an anti-Nazi group, which became known as the *Bekennende Kirche* ('Confessing Church') associated with **Dietrich Bonhoeffer** and Martin Niemöller. Many individuals spoke out against Hitler and took up contacts with others opposed to the regime, such as those involved in the July Plot. Many, like Bonhoeffer, paid with their lives, while others suffered long periods of imprisonment. But prior to 1933 Protestants had generally been more likely to vote for the NSDAP than had Catholics (who remained loyal to the Centre Party), and after 1933 either made their peace with or even supported the regime. German Protestantism was thus deeply divided.

With some individual exceptions, Catholics were neutralised to a considerable extent by the Concordat of July 1933 between the Pope and Hitler. After this, Catholic resistance was, on the whole, defensive: for example, an energetic campaign was mounted against the Nazi proposal to remove crucifixes from schools. Perhaps the major example of at least partially successful resistance came from Bishop Count von Galen of Münster, who in August 1941 preached an outspoken sermon against Hitler's 'euthanasia' programme. Hitler, alarmed by this adverse publicity and always unwilling to risk loss of popularity, put an end to the formal programme of 'euthanasia', although killings continued on a less organised basis.

Active resistance by smaller sects, including notably Quakers, could involve little more than isolated acts of moral courage and witness. Such acts may have saved many individual lives, but were not capable of being effective against the regime in any wider sense. Jehovah's Witnesses were among the targeted victims of the regime.

Groups and individuals against the state

The activities of some individuals and small groups particularly stand out. Among those who took a courageous moral stand were the Munich students, Hans and Sophie Scholl, who, along with one of

Georg Elser (1903–45)

A Swabian carpenter, by late 1938 Elser single-handedly came to the view that Hitler was a dangerous man who must be removed from power. In November 1939, had it not been for Hitler's early departure following his anniversary speech at the Munich Beer Hall, Elser's assassination attempt might well have totally altered the course of history. As it was, however, Elser was arrested, imprisoned in Sachsenhausen concentration camp, and ultimately executed in Dachau in April 1945.

their professors and a small group of friends, formed the *Weisse Rose* group ('White Rose'). They produced and distributed leaflets against the regime, and sought to make contacts with other resistance groups across Germany, but were ultimately caught, arrested, and executed in 1943.

One of the most notable individuals to act entirely on his own (the efforts of both Hitler and subsequently historians to find evidence of wider backing have drawn a blank) was the Swabian carpenter **Georg Elser**. Elser single-mindedly devised a plan to plant a bomb in the Munich Beer Hall, timed to go off when Hitler was positioned right next to it, delivering his annual speech commemorating the failed Beer Hall Putsch of 1923. Elser worked away, night after night, at hollowing out a pillar next to which Hitler would stand. Unfortunately, on the November night in 1939 when the bomb went off, Hitler had one of his famous lucky escapes: the weather being foggy, he had left earlier to take a train back to Berlin rather than going back by plane as originally planned. Elser, who had in the meantime attempted to escape over the border to Switzerland, was caught, imprisoned, and eventually executed in April 1945.

Many individuals assisted in hiding Jews, or seeking to reduce the burden of suffering in some way. They were generally isolated, working under difficult conditions, and easily betrayed. The activities of Oskar Schindler, a highly placed entrepreneur who was initially far from motivated by moral outrage, have been widely publicised in Spielberg's film *Schindler's List*. The apparently successful demonstrations in Berlin's Rosenstrasse by Aryan spouses against the deportation of their Jewish partners have recently been the subject of controversy among historians. Some Jews in mixed marriages were able to survive the genocide, and not only as a result of this particular protest.

Opposition in high places

In theory, those closest to Hitler were best placed to challenge his clearly murderous regime. Here, despite widespread praise, some historians point out that the record is faltering. The late emergence of opposition by leading Army members and those in government circles, among them those who had for some years supported the Nazi regime, along with their generally conservative, anti-democratic ideas of what should replace a Nazi regime, have been criticised by historians such as Hans Mommsen.

Ludwig Beck (1889–1944)

A professional soldier, Beck joined the Army in 1911 and served during the First World War, thereafter rising steadily in the Army hierarchy. From 1935–8 he was Chief of the Army General Staff. He became increasingly worried about Hitler's opportunist tactics and aggressive policies of wars of conquest, and about the growing influence of the Nazi Party over military affairs. Beck resigned his post in August 1938 over Hitler's plans to invade Czechoslovakia, and thereafter was highly active in the German resistance. Had the July Plot succeeded, Beck would have replaced Hitler as Head of State. Instead, however, Beck committed suicide on 20th July 1944.

coup: A sudden violent illegal seizure of government.

For a long time national conservatives went along with Hitler. It was only as Hitler's extreme aims began to differ more openly from those of the traditional elites, in the winter of 1937–8, that well-placed individuals in government, intelligence and Army circles – including **Ludwig Beck**, Hans Oster, Wilhelm Canaris, Franz Halder and Carl Goerdeler – began to think seriously about the possibility of challenging Hitler. Attempts were made to make contact with foreign governments, who tended to remain sceptical, and to discuss ways of removing Hitler from power, or even assassinating him. Following the Munich Conference of 1938, Hitler's domestic popularity was such that ideas for a **coup** were abandoned; and the dramatic military successes of the first two years of the War, alongside the problem of effectively committing treason while the Fatherland was at war, provided further obstacles to nationalist resistance. It was only when the option of an 'honourable' but inevitable defeat seemed preferable to a catastrophic defeat later, that active plans for a coup were resurrected.

The most celebrated plot to topple Hitler, with clear plans for a post-Hitler alternative government, was the so-called 'July Plot' of 1944. **Graf Schenk von Stauffenberg**, sufficiently senior to have close

Claus Graf Schenk von Stauffenberg (1907–1944)

A devout Catholic, Stauffenberg was increasingly disturbed by the immoral character of the Nazi regime, particularly after witnessing the atrocities committed by the SS on the Eastern front. Developing an interest in socialist ideas, Stauffenberg became very active in resistance circles, comparing the ideas for a post-Hitler government of the conservative military resistance (Goerdeler, Beck) with those of the socialist and trade unionist Julius Leber. Stauffenberg devoted himself to the attempt to assassinate Hitler and if possible to replace the Nazis with an alternative government. It was Stauffenberg who unsuccessfully planted the bomb in Hitler's East Prussian headquarters on 20th July 1944. On his return to Berlin (initially unaware that the explosion had not killed Hitler), Stauffenberg was arrested and shot.

access to Hitler, planted a bomb in a briefcase timed to go off whe Hitler was meeting with military planners in his Wolf's Lair retreat i East Prussia. Despite technical problems, Stauffenberg embarked o his return to Berlin with the news of a successful explosio Unfortunately, however, only half the explosives had detonated, an the briefcase had been moved under the protective cover of a ver solid table; Hitler came away with little more than minor injuries an a ruined pair of trousers. The plotters, meanwhile, having been act vated by Stauffenberg's mistaken message, were readily rounded uj along with many others who had been involved in some way wit oppositional activities, and were put to death in a final wave of terrc in 1944–5.

Evaluation

For long periods of time, there were common aims between th Nazi leadership and key elite groups in the economy, the Army, th civil service and among national conservatives. This only began t break down as the regime became more radical in the later 1930 There was also much popular support for certain aspects of th regime. These were strengthened by the Hitler cult, particularly i the 'good times' of economic recovery. There was also widesprea complicity in, and approval of, the regime's treatment of those see to be potentially 'dangerous'. Outright political opposition wa suppressed in a brutal manner very early on. Thereafter, dissent an resistance were isolated. Also important was the increasin fragmentation of society, with the destruction of institutional base for resistance, and significant numbers of people concerne primarily with matters of self-interest, remaining apathetic abou the fate of others.

From a 'fundamentalist' perspective, it is clear that the Na; regime was defeated only by war. The 'societal' interpretation, b contrast, suggests that dissent and nonconformity set limits to th success of the regime's 'total claims'. Moreover, there were som important, if limited, successes in specific areas: the euthanas; programme was at least officially stopped; and, although percentage were small, significant numbers managed to survive persecution i hiding, or to escape through the assistance of courageous opponen of the regime.

Why was there so little internal opposition?

1. Read the following extract and answer the question:

   'A true assessment of the barometer of popular opinion is faced with difficulties at the present time. Because of denunciations, which are still regrettably numerous, and in view of the fanaticism of some subordinate offices, it can be observed that large sections of the population and, in particular, those who are loyal to the State only give vent to their true opinion about public and especially local conditions in their most intimate circle. Otherwise, they simply keep their mouths shut because of completely unjustified fears.'

   (Monthly report of 11 November 1935 by a senior Bavarian government figure, reprinted in Noakes and Pridham (eds.), *Nazism*, Vol. 2, p.569.)

   How useful is this source as an indication of the character of popular opinion in Nazi Germany at the time?

2. *'The main problem with lack of successful opposition to Hitler was not so much that Germans were cowed into obedience by repression, but rather that the vast majority of people, and particularly those in high places, actually agreed with what Hitler was trying to do for Germany. It was only as his policies began to fail that members of the elite started to look for alternatives.'*

   Discuss.

2

Was Hitler responsible for the Second World War?

German foreign policy in international context: Revisionism, Lebensraum, world mastery?

Hitler's role: Master plan or effective opportunism?

In what ways were social and economic developments and foreign policy related?

Framework of events

1933	Germany withdraws from League of Nations' Disarmament Conference
1934	Ten-year non-aggression pact between Germany and Poland
	Death of President Hindenburg
1935	Saar incorporated into Germany
	Stresa Conference between Italy, France and Britain
	France and Russia mutual assistance pact
	British-German naval agreement
	Italy invades Abyssinia
1936	German re-militarisation of the Rhineland
	Four-Year-Plan under Goering
	Anti-Communist pact between Germany and Japan
1938	Nazification of German foreign policy and military leadership
	Anschluss of Austria
	Munich conference: Germany gains Sudetenland
1939	Germany invades Czechoslovakia and seizes Memel
	Germany and Italy sign 'Pact of Steel'
	Germany invades Poland
	Britain and France declare war on Germany in response
1940	German invasion of Denmark, Norway and France
	Italy enters war on the side of Germany
	Franco-German armistice
1941	German invasion of USSR – Operation Barbarossa
	Japanese troops attack Pearl Harbor
	Germany declares war on USA
1943	German defeat at Stalingrad
1945	April 30th: Hitler commits suicide
	German surrender

I T takes more than a single person, and indeed more than a single country, to wage a war. Yet for twenty years or so after the outbreak of the Second World War, the explanation of the War's origins seemed simple enough, and could be condensed into one word: Hitler. An aggressive war of expansion, infused with ideas of racial superiority and the exploitation of 'inferior' peoples appeared so obviously the outcome of the world view presented by Hitler in his 1924 book, *Mein Kampf*, and the war itself appeared to represent so clearly the battle of the forces of good against evil, that it hardly seemed worth looking for further explanation. As A. J. P. Taylor put it in *The Origins of the Second World War* (1961):

> '... an explanation existed which satisfied everybody and seemed to exhaust all dispute. This explanation was: Hitler. He planned the Second World War. His will alone caused it.'

In A. J. P. Taylor's interpretation, by contrast, this Hitler-centric explanation was turned on its head. Hitler – despite his modest social class background and Austrian origins – was recast as a traditional politician pursuing conventional German foreign policy aims. Hitler was however a highly effective opportunist; thus the real problem, according to Taylor, lay in the fact that during the 1930s Hitler was presented with so many opportunities for the revision of Germany's position in Europe. Taylor's account, published in the same year as the German historian Fritz Fischer's controversial reappraisal of the origins of the First World War, raised a storm of controversy. Whether or not Taylor was right in his assessment of earlier historical explanations – which were arguably more varied and complex than he suggested – it is certainly the case that, since the early 1960s, the field has broadened massively, with lively debates over a number of areas.

Landmark Study The book that changed people's views

A. J. P. Taylor, *The Origins of the Second World War* *(Hamish Hamilton, 1961)*

Although now very dated, this highly controversial book remains a classic. Taylor challenged the dominant view of the Second World War as primarily caused by Hitler, a view which remains widespread to this day. He also challenged the view of Hitler as a man driven by clear ideological goals which were single-mindedly pursued through well-formulated plans, a view which is also still widely prevalent today. In Taylor's interpretation, by contrast, Hitler was merely an effective opportunist pursuing traditional German foreign policy aims, but one who, in an increasingly unstable international situation, was faced with unprecedented opportunities for revision and expansion, which he pragmatically exploited as they arose. The book should be read in conjunction with Gordon Martel (ed.), *The Origins of the Second World War Reconsidered* (Routledge, 2nd edn., 1999), which contains key articles summarising current critiques of the Taylor thesis.

German foreign policy in international context: Revisionism, Lebensraum, world mastery?

The Second World War was a highly complex phenomenon. consisted not of one single war, but of many separate conflicts, wit different geographical arenas and periods of conflict across th world. It was preceded by phases of aggression involving mar powers, such as the Spanish Civil War in Europe and conflic involving Japan in the Far East. Many states were also interested i some revision of the European order which had emerged from th Treaty of Versailles. Hitler's role within this broader context international instability is the subject of some disagreement.

Was a Second World War inevitable? The legacies of the Great War

Thirty Years War thesis: The argument that the Second World War was in some respects a continuation of the First World War, with continued flashpoints and unresolved conflicts across Europe in the period 1914–45.

On the one hand, there is what has been dubbed the **Thirty Yea War thesis**, a comparison with the period of sporadic warfan which raged across central Europe in the period 1618–4 According to this view, the 1919 Versailles settlement at the end the 'Great War' of 1914–18 was problematic in so many respec that a further war appeared to be inevitable sooner or later. The had been fundamental alterations to the international balance power, which resulted in a multiplicity of local conflicts ar disputes, along side a lack of genuinely 'national' solutions fe territorial borders, as well as instabilities of the Europea economy. As Marshal Foch, who had been in charge of Alli armies in France in 1918, said of the Treaty of Versailles: 'This not peace. It is an armistice for twenty years.'

There were major shifts in the wider international context a in the character and strengths of the European powers. The US following its late entry into the war, soon retreated in isolationism; it signalled dissatisfaction with the Treaty Versailles as early as November 1919. But the Europe it abandone was very different from that of the pre-war era. The Great War ha wreaked havoc on the economies and politics of the Europea states most directly affected. The newly created communist Sovi Union was economically weak, internally unstable, and politica suspect as far as other powers were concerned. Italy's post-w instability eventuated in the rise of the fascist leader Mussolin who played on a widespread feeling among Italians that in th Versailles settlement they had not received their just rewards f assisting in the defeat of Germany. Britain had both domest

Isolationism: A view prevalent in the USA that it should concern itself solely with its own domestic affairs and not be involved in European conflicts.

social unrest and colonial concerns to worry about. Despite heightened awareness of the horrors of modern warfare after the experience of the trenches and shell-shock on the western front, Britain favoured a degree of revision to the Treaty of Versailles and resumption of friendly relations with Germany. France, also economically weakened and devastated by the loss of so many lives, shared a border with Germany. France was thus most directly concerned about enforcement of the provisions of the Treaty of Versailles, and most worried about future German capacity for aggression. With the disappearance of the Empires of Tsarist Russia, Imperial Germany, and Austria-Hungary, a raft of new 'nation states' were created in central Europe, none of which entirely conformed with notions of national boundaries. Thus there were countless disputed borders and potential flashpoints, from Vilna and Memel through Silesia and the Sudetenland to the Rhineland and South Tyrol.

Finally, to this catalogue should be added the economic consequences of the war. Some were unavoidable, others (notably in the case of the German inflation of 1923), were made very much worse by deliberate government policies of exacerbating pre-existing trends. Widespread unwillingness to accept the territorial, military, political and economic provisions of the Treaty of Versailles, as well as the 'national humiliation' it allegedly entailed, was also highly visible in Germany.

If this view of general international instability is correct, Hitler was merely the person who happened to be in charge of Germany when the inevitable erruption happened. He might have added colour and detail to the shape of events, but could not be held to be the primary or sole cause of war. Without the First World War, there would, as Kershaw has cogently argued, have been no Hitler. The logic of those adhering to the 'Thirty Years' War thesis' is to suggest that even without Hitler, there would have been a Second World War.

Against this view, many historians argue that there were in fact successful measures for stabilisation of the international system in 1920s. The **Locarno Treaty** of 1925 regularised and recognised Germany's western borders, providing a degree of German assent to the 'Diktat' of Versailles in this area. **The League of Nations**, and Germany's entry into it in 1926, appeared to provide an international framework for the peaceful resolution of disputes. Finally, the **Dawes Plan** of 1924, and the **Young Plan** of 1929 which replaced it, seemed to offer realistic measures for dealing with reparations. Revision of the Treaty of Versailles was thus on the international

---

he Locarno reaty, 1925: A treaty etween Germany, France, elgium, Italy and Britain, uaranteeing the western rontiers of Germany with rance and Belgium. lthough Germany ncluded separate greements with echoslovakia and Poland, e 1926 Berlin Treaty tween Germany and ssia left Poland in a lnerable position and the estion of Germany's stern frontiers remained en.

he League of ations: based on US esident Wilson's 'fourteen ints' of 1918, this was t up in 1919 as part of e Versailles settlement 'to ate mutual guarantees of e political independence d territorial integrity of tes, large and small ually'. Germany was nitted in 1926, and hdrew in 1933.

awes Plan/Young an: the Dawes Plan of 24 regularised Germany's arations payments in e short term. The Young n of 1929 was designed be a final settlement of much reduced arations bill, to be paid er 59 years.

Wall Street Crash of 1929: following years of rising investment on the American stock market in New York's Wall Street, a sudden loss of confidence precipitated a spiral of selling and dramatic losses in share prices in October 1929. The resulting bankruptcies occasioned massive unemployment and inaugurated years of economic depression in the USA, with reverberations across Europe, most marked in Germany, which had been dependent on short-term loans from the USA.

Revisionism: the view that the Treaty of Versailles was in need of revision.

Hitler's programme: the notion among some historians that Hitler had clearly formulated aims and plans to achieve his goals, which he then pursued single-mindedly.

Congruence of aims: specific areas over which different groups agreed with Hitler about desired ends, without necessarily accepting much, if any, of the wider ideological baggage of Nazism.

agenda and peaceful adjustments were not impossible in principl From this perspective, the international situation might well hav stabilised with peaceful resolution of disputed issues, had it n been for the **Wall Street Crash of 1929**, the consequent plunge int Depression and the related rise of ideological movements, of whic the most virulently aggressive was Nazism in Germany.

What did the rise of Hitler add to this unstable situation?

Revisionism now came to play an important role in a rath different way. In the context of economic crisis after 1929, wid spread resentment at Germany's 'national humiliation' aft Versailles could be linked with the hatred whipped up by Nazi pro agenda of the so-called 'November criminals'. The Nazis claime that the 'Bolsheviks' and 'Jews' had conspired to 'stab Germany i the back', resulting in the loss of the war.

To the traditional revisionist demands were now added t Hitler's views on the 'master race' and its alleged need f *Lebensraum* ('living space'). Thus began a policy not merely revision but also of aggressive expansion, colonisation of ne territories in eastern Europe, and ultimately perhaps even wor domination. In his political tract *Mein Kampf*, written while i Landsberg prison in 1924 and published in 1925, and in h unpublished *Second Book* of 1928, Hitler presented foreign poli aims which, linked intrinsically to his rabid racism, seemed to g way beyond those of traditional revisionism.

Whichever view is held of international instability, Hitler's aim did seem to add new ingredients to the equation. Yet even the ro of **Hitler's programme** is disputed.

Hitler's role: master plan or effective opportunism?

If Taylor was reacting against an undue emphasis on Hitler as th primary cause, then soon there was in turn a reaction, with Hitler intentions brought right back into centre stage. Revisionism w clearly a key element in the so-called **congruence of aims** betwee the Nazi leadership and conservative nationalist elites in Germany without which Hitler would not have come to power. According t some historians, however, Hitler had clearly defined and mo radical goals, or a 'master plan', which continually guided h actions and informed his strategies as events unfolded.

Hitler's Programme?

The notion that Hitler was operating according to a master plan or pre-conceived programme, rooted in a consistent and strongly held *Weltanschauung* ('world view') was argued most fully by a number of German historians in the late 1960s and early 1970s.

Andreas Hillgruber argued in *Germany and the Two World Wars* (1967) that during the 1920s Hitler developed 'a firm program, to which he then single-mindedly adhered until his suicide in the Reich Chancellery on April 30, 1945.' This programme entailed a 'stage plan': first, Germany would gain control of continental Europe and colonise Russia in order to gain *Lebensraum*. Germany would then become a world power with African colonies and a strong navy (on a par with Britain, Japan and the USA). Finally, probably after Hitler's own lifetime, Germany would engage in a 'battle of the continents', fighting the USA for world domination. The scheme was further infused with racist ideology, linking Bolshevism and **'international Jewry'**, both of which were targets for destruction.

According to Eberhard Jaeckel in *Hitler's World View: A Blueprint for Power* (1969), by the time of writing his secret *Second Book* of 1928, Hitler had developed a 'grand design' which then remained his guiding plan. Jaeckel claims: 'Few statesmen have ever pursued their goals with greater obstinacy or tenacity' Klaus Hildebrand in *The Foreign Policy of the Third Reich* (1973), agrees that the ultimate aim of Hitler's 'Programme' (which he dignifies with a capital 'P') was and remained 'world domination based on race'.

Some historians, however, dispute the coherence of Hitler's views, pointing to the inconsistencies, gaps and poor judgements in his thinking. These historians doubt that Hitler's rag-bag of prejudices really amounted to a 'master plan', with any serious strategy for translating megalomaniac fantasies into actual practice. Nor is it easy to assess the evidence of Hitler's speeches and writings. A quotation can be found to support virtually every side of the argument; but the significance of such quotations is far more difficult to determine. A. J. P. Taylor was highly sceptical of using Hitler's words as evidence. In *The Origins of the Second World War* (1961) he claims:

> 'If his talk of peace was play-acting, so also was his talk of war. Which would become real depended on events, not on any resolution taken by Hitler beforehand.'

Moreover, Hitler did not operate in a vacuum. To identify a coherent plan from Hitler's utterances and writings is not necessarily to

'International Jewry': Hitler's vague and ideologically loaded term for an assumed international network of Jews, who were allegedly behind both 'Bolshevism' and 'international finance capitalism'.

demonstrate that it was his own ideas that actually determined the course of German foreign policy in the 1930s.

Hitler was also to some extent a product of his time. The quest for *Lebensraum* within central and particularly eastern Europe was not unique to Nazism: concepts of some form of German domination of *Mitteleuropa* ('Central European Area') had been under active discussion among German nationalist circles for some time. Notions of access to *Lebensraum* in central Europe were built on the view that political boundaries were not natural frontiers fixed for eternity, but were rather the product of struggles for command over valuable land and resources. Similarly, a notion of racial superiority, although most virulent in Nazism was shared by many European elites. The imperialist adventures of France and Britain were based on the view that it was entirely permissible to exploit other areas of the world, and to export the culture of the colonial power to native peoples whose own customs were held to be inferior.

Hitler's role must also be seen in the context of the changing character of government and the development of the Hitler state. There were multiple variants of foreign policy visions and views present throughout the 1930s, and to a greater or lesser extent these informed German policy-making at different moments during this time. However, there was a distinct shift (and radicalisation) of those in a position of power to translate views into policy from the mid-1930s onwards.

'Congruence of aims'?

In the early years of the Third Reich, the Army, the Foreign Office and the Nazi Party were largely in agreement over the need for revision of the Treaty of Versailles. Plans for rearmament were discussed within the first weeks of Hitler's Chancellorship. In October 1933 German withdrew from the Disarmament Conference in Geneva and Hitler announced Germany's intention to withdraw from the League of Nations. By January 1934 a worried Poland concluded a ten-year non aggression pact with Germany. But when in the summer of 1934 crisis arose following the murder of Austrian Chancellor Dollfuss by Austrian Nazis, Mussolini's mobilisation of Italian troops at the Italian border with Austria was sufficient to diffuse the situation for the time being.

The German threat, however, continued to grow, prompting further jostling for what proved to be rather unstable alliances. On 9 March 1935, Goering revealed the existence of a German air

ussolini welcomes Hitler
Italy during his state
sit, May 1938.

force – which had been expressly forbidden under the Versailles Treaty – and a week later universal military conscription was announced. In April, representatives from Britain, France and Italy met at the Italian resort of Stresa and condemned German rearmament. The unanimity of the Stresa Front was, however, short-lived. Neither Britain nor Italy were happy about France concluding a treaty with communist Russia in May 1935; and the British naval agreement with Germany, concluded in June 1935, was a clear signal that Britain was prepared to condone breaches of the Treaty if this seemed in Britain's interests. In the autumn of 1935, somewhat inconsistent and vacillating responses on the part of both France and Britain to the Italian invasion of Abyssinia led ultimately to economic sanctions against Italy. These sanctions signalled the break-up of the Stresa front and, curiously, a degree of rapprochement between Germany and Italy.

The radicalisation of foreign policy

Radicalisation can be observed from 1936 onwards, with increasing Nazi control of the economy, foreign policy and military planning. Hitler gained a pivotal role in the determining of both the aims and methods of foreign policy, apparently providing clear evidence of putting a 'programme' into practice. Yet Hitler's plans were not all achieved, and his methods were often highly opportunistic, seizing favourable moments and exploiting sudden turns in events to his own advantage.

In early 1936, Hitler chose to act on the question of the Rhineland, a demilitarised zone under the provisions of the Treaty of Versailles. The remilitarisation of the Rhineland had long been on the general revisionist agenda, although traditionalists would have preferred this to be negotiated through normal diplomatic channels. Hitler, however, unsettled by loss of popular support within Germany, and concerned to maintain his image as the charismatic *Führer*, wanted a more spectacular achievement.

Hitler saw a brief window of opportunity offered by Italy's invasion of Abyssinia (a war he managed to assist in prolonging by sending arms to the Abyssinian resistance to Mussolini's troops). Choosing a more high profile approach, Hitler, in March 1936 sent in German troops, confident that the French would offer little resistance. Events proved this strategy correct: the French failed to meet the fairly minimal German display of force with any serious counter-force, and the British treated the Germans' action as little more than re-entering their 'own back garden'. Hitler scored a major propaganda coup and his domestic popularity soared.

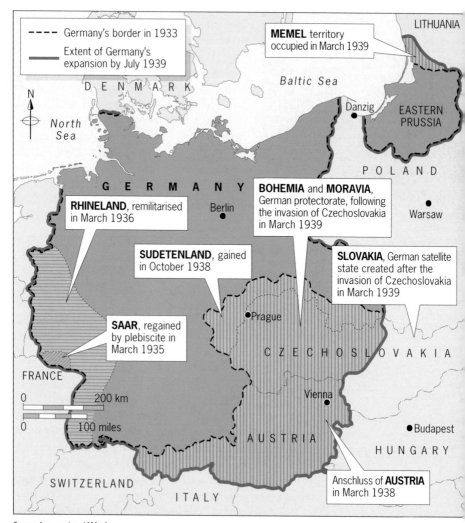

- - - Germany's border in 1933

—— Extent of Germany's expansion by July 1939

MEMEL territory occupied in March 1939

RHINELAND, remilitarised in March 1936

BOHEMIA and **MORAVIA**, German protectorate, following the invasion of Czechoslovakia in March 1939

SUDETENLAND, gained in October 1938

SLOVAKIA, German satellite state created after the invasion of Czechoslovakia in March 1939

SAAR, regained by plebiscite in March 1935

Anschluss of **AUSTRIA** in March 1938

Germany's expansion, 1933–9.

**Hjalmar Schacht
(1877–1970)**

An economics graduate and financial expert, Schacht was in charge of stabilising the German currency in the inflationary crisis of 1923, and was involved in negotiating the Dawes Plan of 1924 and the Young Plan of 1929. Increasingly disillusioned by Weimar politics, Schacht helped to gain support for Hitler among financial and industrial circles in 1932–3. He became Minister of Economics in 1934, contributing greatly to Germany's economic recovery and early rearmament. Disagreeing with Goering's policies of autarchy under the Four Year Plan, Schacht resigned as Minister of Economics in 1937. In his capacity as President of the Reichsbank in 1938–9, Schacht sought to organise a plan for the emigration of German Jews. Increasing disaffection with Hitler led to contacts with resistance circles, and following the failure of the 1944 July Plot Schacht was imprisoned. Acquitted at the Nuremberg trials, Schacht was able to enjoy a long and lucrative retirement in the Federal Republic of Germany.

In spring 1936, there were shortages of meat, butter, raw materials and foreign exchange in Germany. Despite these shortages, Hitler announced that he wanted to be ready for war 'within four years', with no adverse effects on domestic consumption. Against the advice of the Ministry of Economics under **Hjalmar Schacht**, Hitler abandoned liberal economic doctrines and authorised Goering to increase armaments production under the auspices of the new Four-Year-Plan Office, set up in August 1936. Schacht was forced to resign in November 1937.

**Wilhelm Keitel
(1882–1946)**

A professional soldier, Keitel took on the post of Chief of Staff of the High Command of the Armed Forces following the purge of the Army leadership in February 1938. An adulating supporter of Hitler, Keitel played a major role in ensuring that the Army assisted the SS, and justified the implementation of terror and mass murder in the occupied territories on the eastern front. He was found guilty by the Nuremberg Tribunal and executed in October 1946.

The outbreak of the Spanish Civil War in 1936 increasingly polarised opinion in Europe. Nazi Germany and fascist Italy intervened on behalf of the nationalist rebels under Spain's General Franco, who had risen against the left-wing Spanish Republican government coalition in Spain, while Russia and Communists across Europe supported the Republicans. In the course of 1936–7, Germany and Italy became closer in the Rome-Berlin Axis, while the attempts of Hitler's Nazi agent in London, Joachim von Ribbentrop, to gain an alliance with Britain seemed to be leading nowhere. Japan now began to look like a more suitable ally.

By 1937, the German re-armament programme was causing tensions between the conflicting priorities of the Army, Navy and Air Force. Army leaders were concerned about potential social unrest; and they were rattled by Hitler's increasingly strident tone with respect to foreign policy, captured in the 'Hossbach memorandum' of November 1937. In the spring of 1938 the Army leadership was purged. War Minister Werner von Blomberg was dismissed, and the War Ministry was replaced by a new High Command of the Armed Forces (OKW) under **Wilhelm Keitel** a unique arrangement in a peacetime state. The Commander-in-Chief of the Army, Werner von Fritsch was ousted and replaced by General Walther von Brauchitsch. Hitler himself assumed a more prominent military role as Commander-in-Chief of the Armed Forces. The Foreign Ministry was also 'Nazified', with Foreign Minister Konstantin von Neurath replaced by Joachim von Ribbentrop.

In 1938–9 foreign policy moved into a radically new gear, with Hitler both creating and manipulating new opportunities in a rapid escalation of diplomatic and military action. Austrian Chancellor von Schnuschnigg was summonsed to Hitler's Alpine retreat at Berchtesgaden in March 1938, and forced into giving the post of Austrian Minister of the Interior to a Nazi. When von Schuschnigg nevertheless called a plebiscite on whether or not to maintain Austrian independence, Hitler mobilised the German army. With no moves on the part of Italy, France or Britain to defend Austria, on 11 March 1938 German troops were able to march into Austria unopposed. Hitler returned triumphant to his home town of Linz, and announced the *Anschluss* ('union') of Germany and Austria.

Having encountered no serious international opposition to revision of German borders, Hitler next turned his attentions to the Sudetenland area of Czechoslovakia, where unrest among ethnic Germans had been stirred up by the local Nazi leader. With Hitler designating 1 October 1938 as a date for military invasion, the Army Chief of Staff, General Beck, and others in government and intelligence circles began to feel uneasy, and plans for a possible coup were seriously discussed at high levels for the first time.

Fate now intervened in the form of British Prime Minister Neville Chamberlain, whose policies of 'appeasement' have occasioned much historical controversy. Braving the rigours of modern travel by aeroplane, Chamberlain met Hitler at Berchtesgaden and again in the rapidly convened Munich Conference in September 1938. Britain, France, Italy and Germany – in the absence of representatives from both Russia and Czechoslovakia (the country directly affected) – tried to avert war by conceding German demands. Hitler, infuriated that he had been cheated of his planned war, was nevertheless emboldened. In March 1939 German troops invaded the now militarily weakened state of Czechoslovakia and a week later they seized the Lithuanian port of Memel.

In the meantime, however, Britain had been rapidly rearming and on some views the time for effective rearmament had been bought by the policy of appeasement. On 31 March 1939, Britain offered a guarantee to Poland that it would come to Poland's defence if there were any further German moves of aggression.

Pact of Steel: Signed
on 22 May 1939, this
created a military alliance
between Germany and Italy
in the event of war, and
confirmed Italy's break
with France and Britain.

Hitler, who had failed to obtain his desired alliance with Britain, concluded a **Pact of Steel** with Mussolini in May. Russia was wooed both by the western powers (who needed Russian help to prevent German expansion eastwards), and by Hitler, who had no desire to fight a war on two fronts. In the event, in late August 1939 the German-Soviet non-aggression pact, arranged by Joachim von Ribbentrop, with its provisions for a carve-up of Poland between Russia and Germany, gave Germany the green light for the invasion of Poland on 1 September 1939. Honouring its guarantee, on 3 September the British government announced that it was now at war with Germany.

Hitler's strategies shaped not only the outbreak but also the course of the war. His most fateful interventions were the ideologically loaded invasion of 'Bolshevik' Russia in the summer of 1941, and the declaration of war on the mighty USA following the Japanese attack on the American base at Pearl Harbor in December 1941. It is these acts that transformed a European War into a World War.

In what ways were social and economic developments and foreign policy related?

The Third Reich was inherently unstable, built on a policy of drive and dynamism. From its inception, the Third Reich was geared to prepare for war – and rearmament carried major implications for economic and social developments. These, in turn, arguably conditioned the character of foreign policy and the nature of the war which resulted. Hitler's own popularity was also closely related to developments in foreign policy.

Popular opinion and foreign policy

Hitler constantly had an eye on his personal standing with the German people: as we have seen, much of his support was rooted in the 'Hitler myth'. To remain a national saviour figure above the strains and strife of daily life required him to deliver the goods, and do so in a way that did not upset significant sections of the population. Such considerations, while never entirely deflecting Hitler from his principal aims, certainly played a role in foreign policy developments. Conversely, the developments in foreign policy affected Hitler's own standing in the popularity stakes.

Public opinion was less directly relevant to a dictatorial government than to a democratic government, as in the cases of France and Britain, whose economic policies in relation to rearmament had to have a constant eye on potential social unrest. Fear of consumer dissatisfaction nevertheless played a major role in Hitler's thinking with respect to economic policy. Domestic considerations also affected the timing and character of some foreign policy developments, as in the case of the re-militarisation of the Rhineland.

On the occasion of the Munich Conference in 1938, Hitler himself felt cheated of a planned war, but German public opinion appeared mighty relieved that imminent war had been averted and that Germany had made a significant foreign policy gain by peaceful means.

The economy and foreign policy

Autobahn system: the network of motorways across Germany.

Volksgemeinschaft: the supposedly harmonious and racially defined 'people's community' or 'folk community', which Hitler claimed to be constructing in Germany in place of a modern society riven by class conflicts.

The German economy was deeply affected both by the drive for rearmament and the demands of war. It was further complicated by Hitler's concern not to compromise standards of living and hence his own popularity. Economic recovery had set in already in late 1932, although from 1933 it was enhanced by rearmament-related initiatives. Work creation schemes and prestige projects such as the building of the German **autobahn system** were designed not merely to tackle unemployment, but to raise a sense of national pride in the ***Volksgemeinschaft***. In addition, they were important in developing a basic preparedness for war. Rearmament was not a major concern

Hermann Goering at the opening celebrations for the three planned *Reichswerke*, 1938.

at this time, accounting for perhaps only 18 per cent of expenditure in work creation schemes in the period 1932–4; but from the mid-1930s onwards it became increasingly important.

By 1936 there was a growing economic crisis, causing political tensions. The Minister of Economics, Hjalmar Schacht, wanted to scale down the escalating costs; but Hitler was unwilling either to abandon plans for rapid rearmament or to risk consumer dissatisfaction. This led directly to the break with orthodox economic planning, and the creation of Goering's new Four-Year-Plan office. This was a typical illustration of the polycratic character of the regime, where if Hitler was not satisfied with one quarter, he simply empowered someone else to deal with the issue. It also meant radically increased state intervention in the economy. From 1936 onwards, preparation for 'war within four years' meant attempting to square the economic circle: to combine a high standard of living with the demands of rapid arms production.

By 1938–9, rearmament expenditure had risen by 70 per cent above the level of the previous two years. The focus was now on autarchy (self-sufficiency) rather than reliance on imports from abroad. In part this required the enhanced production of synthetics, or substitutes for raw materials which could no longer be obtained from elsewhere. In part it also entailed a shift to exploitation of the resources of other countries, including Austria after the Anschluss, and Czechoslovakia following the invasion, as well as bilateral agreements with other countries such as Romania, an important supplier of oil. Consumption as a percentage of national income declined from 71 per cent in 1928 to 59 per cent in 1938, although domestic unrest was not as great as might have been expected under a democratic regime. Certain sections of business were adversely affected by the shift to autarchy and increased state intervention, although it operated to the advantage of sectors engaged in the production of synthetics, such as I. G. Farben.

Economic developments had implications for the timing and character of the war. According to the opinions of some historians, from 1936 onwards the economy became increasingly 'unhinged'. They argue that it entailed going to war sooner rather than later, and shaped the nature of the war that could be fought. In principle, the economy could in future only be sustained by a successful war of conquest, acquiring and exploiting further territories as the need arose, as Hitler himself believed. However, because of the speed and type of rearmament, Germany would not be ready for major war until the mid-1940s. Until then, all Germany could prepare for were 'lightning strikes' or a *Blitzkrieg* style of warfare evident in the early months of the war. By contrast, both Britain and France would I militarily prepared for war by 1939.

These developments also had major implications for Germa society. Germans in the concentration camps were deployed as sla labour, working in appalling conditions such as in the quarries Mauthausen, or in the growing empire of SS industrial enterprise Despite Nazi ideology on the role of women, who supposed belonged in the spheres of 'children, kitchen, church', by 1939 52 p cent of women of working age were in employment. Increasing foreign labour was brought into Germany to assist in production. A these trends developed massively during the war itself.

What difference, then, did Hitler make?

Many foreign policy developments of the 1930s might have con about under any conservative nationalist and revisionist goverr ment. Rearmament and the revision of Germany's boundaries defined in the Treaty of Versailles were shared very widely. Yet it wa Hitler's interference in, and radicalisation of, foreign policy whic made a crucial difference in several respects.

Hitler's foreign policy goals were a top priority for him, drivir alterations to the domestic power structure. His determination press on with rearmament at all costs, altered the balance betwee the Nazi party, the state and the Army. It also greatly increased sta intervention in a changing economy. The rearmament programn affected the timing and character of the war which Germany ult mately fought. It hence conditioned, although it did not necessari predetermine, the outcome of the war.

In terms of the involvement of particular combatants, Hitl failed to gain an alliance with Britain. He turned a war again Russia into one of extraordinary ideological aggression and raci hatred. He also brought the previously isolationist USA int European affairs in a way which was to be of major long-term signi icance for twentieth-century European and world history. Finally, was in the midst of this conflagration that the Holocaust wa unleashed.

Was he responsibie for the Second World War?

1. Read the following extract and answer the question:

   'The second World war was, in large part, a repeat performance of the first ... Germany fought specifically in the second war to reverse the verdict of the first and to destroy the settlement which followed it ... The first war explains the second and, in fact, caused it, in so far as one event causes another.'

   (A. J. P. Taylor, *The Origins of the Second World War,* Hamish Hamilton, 1961, pp. 18–9.)

   To what extent, if at all, do you agree with this interpretation of the causes of the Second World War?

2. Assess the character and implications of German economic policies during the period 1933–9 in preparing for war.

3

The Holocaust: How did Nazi racial policies turn into genocide?

How important were Hitler's intentions within the context of the Nazi state structures?

How can we explain the 'cumulative radicalisation' of racial policies from 1933 to 1941?

To what extent were 'ordinary Germans' responsible for the Holocaust?

Framework of events

1933	Boycott of Jewish shops
	'Law for the Restitution of the Professional Civil Service'
	Sterilisation of persons with 'hereditary illness'
1935	Nuremberg Laws
1936	Olympics in Berlin
1938	*Anschluss* and exacerbation of anti-Semitism in Austria
	9 November: *Kristallnacht*
	Aryanisation of Jewish businesses
	Pressures for emigration
1939	Invasion of Poland and mass killings of Polish elites
	'Resettlement' plans: a 'territorial solution'? (Lublin, Madagascar)
	The euthanasia programme in Germany (1939–41)
1941	Plans for 'Barbarossa' – racial and political war against '*Untermenschen*'
	'Commissary order'
	Invasion of Russia
	Einsatzgruppen enter Russia
	Rapid escalation of numbers involved and numbers killed
	3 September: test of Zyklon B gas
	Emigration prohibited, overcrowding of ghettos
	Gassings at Chelmno
	12 December: Hitler announces mass killings to party leaders
1942	January: Wannsee conference co-ordinates mass murder
	Major extermination camps constructed: Auschwitz II (Birkenau), Sobibor, Treblinka, Belzec Majdanek
1942–45	Holocaust continues until German defeat in 1945

Nazi Germany was not the first or only racist state. Although Nazi racial policies were not rooted in a background of slavery, initially they bore some similarities to policies of apartheid in South Africa and segregation in the USA. Yet when Nazi policies developed into mass murder they were ultimately far more severe. Nazi policies of genocide have been compared with the mass killings perpetrated by Stalin in the USSR and Pol Pot in Cambodia, provoking considerable controversy over possible 'relativisation' of the Holocaust.

The word 'Holocaust' is something of a misnomer for the organised murder of millions of human beings by the Nazi regime. 'Holocaust', or the Jewish term *Shoah*, means literally a 'burnt sacrifice'. Yet despite being an ill-fitting term the word 'Holocaust' has come to stick. Genocide was linked to the wider attempt to create a racially pure 'folk community' (*Volksgemeinschaft*). The majority of victims of the Holocaust were murdered on grounds of race: most notably the Jews, and also almost the entire European population of Sinti and Roma (gypsies). But other groups were also targets, including homosexuals, Jehovah's Witnesses, communists, socialists, individual Christians and any others who stood up to Hitler. It is estimated that perhaps six million people – women and men, young and old – lost their lives in this systematic, bureaucratically organised or **'industrial' genocide.**

industrial' genocide: organised mass murder of large numbers of people by technologically advanced means in specially designed and constructed extermination centres or 'factories of death'

How important were Hitler's intentions within the context of the Nazi state structures?

Until the early 1960s, the Holocaust played little role in historiography. It came to prominence with the **Adolf Eichmann** trial in Jerusalem and the Auschwitz trial in Frankfurt, when the centrality of 'Hitler and his henchmen' remained more or less

Adolf Eichmann (1906–62)

Eichmann was in charge of Nazi emigration, evacuation and eventually extermination policies. He joined the Austrian Nazi party in 1932, and in 1934 he found a job in Himmler's SD, where by 1935 he was in charge of 'Jewish questions'. Following the *Anschluss* in 1938, Eichmann returned to Austria and ran the 'Office for Jewish Emigration' in Vienna, organising the forced exit of 150 000 Jews within eighteen months. In 1939, Eichmann was moved to the RSHA to deal with Jewish 'evacuations', and from 1941 the 'resettlement' policies that were ultimately to end in the extermination camps. Following the Wannsee Conference, Eichmann had the task of bureaucratic implementation of the 'Final Solution'. After the war, he managed to escape to Argentina; he was only finally discovered in 1960 and removed to Israel, where he stood trial in Jerusalem in 1961. He was found guilty and executed in 1962.

Hans Globke (1898–1973)
A civil servant in the Reich Ministry of the Interior, Globke wrote, along with Wilhelm Stuckart, the official commentary on the Nuremberg Race Laws which excluded German Jews from full citizenship rights. He was also involved in further 'legal' aspects of the persecution of Jews and the 'Germanisation' of occupied territories. Globke retained his position as a civil servant in the new post-war Federal Republic of Germany, employed in the capacity of State Secretary of the Chancellory as the chief aide to Konrad Adenauer, the first West German Chancellor, until his retirement in 1963.

taken for granted. But with the rise of wider debates ove Hitler's role in the structures of power (see *Hitler, Book 1* new twists developed. In the 1970s and 1980s a debate aros between the so-called intentionalists and the structuralis (functionalists).

The intentionalists emphasise Hitler's 'programme' (as i the works of Hildebrand, Hillgruber and Jaeckel): Hitler murderous aims were translated into policies and practice a opportunities arose; there was a direct line from the ant Semitism of *Mein Kampf* to the gas chambers of Auschwitz. I *The War against the Jews* (1975), Lucy Dawidowicz argue that the Holocaust resulted from Hitler's 'fundamental belie and ideological conviction'; the link 'between idea and act ha seldom been as evident in human history with such manifes consistency'. Gerald Fleming claims that there was a 'singl unbroken and fatal continuum' between Hitler's early ant Semitic outpourings and 'the liquidation orders that Hitle personally issued during the war' (*Hitler and the Fin Solution*, 1985).

There is no doubt about Hitler's anti-Semitism. He share the view, widespread among right-wing circles (and not on in Germany), that the Jews were not merely a religious grou but also were racially distinct. Religious and cultural ant Semitism had been prevalent for centuries. The racial versio of anti-Semitism, a product of the new scientific theories c the nineteenth century, added a whole new dimension to th question. It meant that the Jewish Question could not b solved by conversion or assimilation: even if Jews renounce Judaism and converted to Christianity, they would still b irredeemably 'Jewish'. Hitler believed that this constituted danger to the health of the *Volksgemeinschaft*, and compared Jev with a physical disease which had to be removed.

Hitler made numerous statements to this effect. Raging again 'Jewish Bolsheviks' and 'International Jewry' had been part of h stock-in-trade with the party faithful from the early 1920s, an repeated frequently, most notably in the hideous 'prophecy' made i a speech to the Reichstag on 30 January 1939 (see exam question In subsequent references to his Reichstag 'prophecy', Hitler himse wrongly dated it to the outbreak of war in September 1939. Th connection between war and the 'Jewish question' was of grea significance.

But do Hitler's anti-Semitic utterances constitute evidence of clear 'programme' that intrinsically meant, and had to mean, ma:

murder? And are Hitler's views a sufficient explanation of the transition from racial policies into genocide?

The functionalists argue that there was not a direct connection between Hitler's intentions and murderous outcome, but rather that there was a 'twisted road' (Karl Schleunes' phrase) to Auschwitz. Only the curious structures of power in the polycratic state explain how the crazy ideas of one man became mass murder by many.

Far from being a streamlined totalitarian state, in which Hitler's orders were simply turned into realities, functionalists argue that there were multiple, overlapping centres of power. Hans Mommsen and Martin Broszat argue that, while Hitler set the broad agenda, the 'cumulative radicalisation' of racial policy can be explained in terms of competition among underlings in ever more difficult circumstances. Genocide was the result of improvisation, of a continued search for new solutions, as the self-made problem of the 'Jewish question' became ever more acute. While not down-playing the role of Hitler, greater emphasis is given here to decision-making at the local level. In the wider context of Hitler's aim of making German-occupied Europe 'free of Jews' (*Judenfrei*, or *Judenrein*), ever more radical local initiatives were taken to 'cleanse' particular areas of Jews. Mass murder was a relatively late solution to an ever-growing 'problem', rather than planned from the outset and instigated by an order from on high once conditions were right.

Theoretical interpretations have shifted somewhat in recent years. Moderate approaches have combined a focus on Hitler's intentions with an awareness of the importance of local initiatives and improvisation on the ground (examples, which disagree over detail, include the works of Philippe Burrin and Christopher Browning). Ian Kershaw has picked up on a phrase uttered by a contemporary, 'working towards the *Führer*', to combine recognition of the polycratic structures of the regime with the centrality of Hitler's role. New debates have opened up on questions such as the extent to which Nazi racial policies were the product of 'modernity', social engineering, and 'scientific' **eugenic theories**. The roles of the **planning intelligentsia** and other technocrats have been emphasised, as has the role of the Army alongside the SS.

ugenic theories: eories about the genetic hereditary aracteristics of a pulation, often companied by policies signed to 'improve' the ock'.

lanning telligentsia: a term ed by some historians to note the groups involved technical planning in lation to matters such as pulation policy and ving space'.

Iow can we explain the 'cumulative radicalisation' of acial policies from 1933 to 1941?

While very few individuals (apart from extreme right-wing Holocaust deniers) dispute the established facts, controversies over

interpretation continue to rage: revisiting the chronology is essentia
to explore these debates further.

Discrimination and stigmatisation in a 'racial state', 1933–7

In the early 1930s, German Jews were simply Germans who wer
Jewish. Many had married Christian or non-religious Germans
producing children whom Nazis categorised as *'Mischlinge'* ('thos
of mixed descent'). As Victor Klemperer, a Jewish German married t
a non-Jewish German, noted in his diary in January 1939: 'Until 193.
and for at least a good century before that, the German Jews wer
entirely German and nothing else. Proof: the thousands an
thousands of half- and quarter-Jews etc.' The identification of Germa
Jews as distinctively different required a phase of stigmatisation, i
the context of the wider policies of a racial state.

'Mischlinge': the Nazi racist term for people of 'mixed' parentage, for example children of 'mixed marriages' where perhaps two of their four grandparents were Jewish.

A boycott of Jewish shops and businesses took place at th
beginning of April 1933, largely as a result of pressures on the part c
Nazi party radicals. Finding that this met with popular disapprova
Hitler rapidly called off the action. Yet within days came a mor
legalistic approach to discrimination, in the form of the 'Law for th
Restitution of the Professional Civil Service'. This excluded Jews
communists, socialists, and other 'undesirables' from a broad rang
of professional jobs. The legalisation of discrimination appears t
have been met with widespread acquiescence lack of protest. In th
following months, further measures to redesign German societ
along racial lines were taken. Compulsory sterilisation of thos
considered unsuitable to reproduce on grounds of supposedl
hereditary diseases, disabilities and other conditions (includin
chronic alcoholism and 'asocial' behaviour) were introduced. Racisn
began to enter all areas of everyday life: hideous images of Jew
represented as extremely greedy, sexually menacing, hook-nosed an
untrustworthy, or metaphorically akin to dangerous germs o
vermin were present not only in obvious propaganda outlets
but also in encyclopaedias, medical dictionaries, books on art o
literature, and children's schoolbooks.

The Nuremberg Race Laws of 1935 illustrate the relative signifi
cance of the various pressures from party radicals, popular opinior
civil servants, and Hitler's role within a particular structure of powe
By the summer of 1935 Nazi party radicals were becoming restless
while law-abiding Germans disapproved of random acts of violence
Concerned both to maintain personal popularity and to appease part
radicals, Hitler resorted to further legalisation of discrimination. A

Landmark Study   **The book that changed people's views**

Raul Hilberg, *The Destruction of the European Jews* (Holmes and Meier: original 1961, revised edn., 3 vols, 1985)

It is almost impossible to nominate a single 'landmark study' in a subject as contested and complex as that of Nazi racial policies and the Holocaust. However, despite the wealth of possible candidates in this field, Hilberg's massive work, first published in 1961 and revised in the 1980s, gains the 'landmark' accolade here, simply for being one of the very first to attempt, doggedly and persistently, the mammoth task of trying to record what actually happened, and how precisely it happened. In his own words, he tried 'to explore the sheer mechanism of destruction' at a time when 'the academic world was oblivious to the subject, and publishers found it unwelcome' (p. ix, p. xi).

the Nuremberg party rally in September 1935, he announced the so-called Nuremberg Laws, which were hastily drafted by civil servants flown in from Berlin. With the Reich Citizenship Law, Jewish Germans were reduced to second-class citizenship. Mixed marriages were forbidden under the Law for the Protection of German Blood and German Honour, as was the employment of German women under the age of 45 in Jewish households. It then took several weeks for civil servants in Berlin to fight out among themselves the details of who precisely was to count as a Jew. Hitler typically sided with the emergent winner. The slightly more lenient definition of Jewishness won out, conforming neither to a strictly religious nor a strictly racial definition. Individuals with three or four Jewish grandparents were held to be Jews, while '*Mischlinge*' with two Jewish grandparents were considered Jewish if they practised Judaism or married a Jew, and not Jewish if they did not. Under this definition, there were approximately 502 000 full Jews and around 200 000 *Mischlinge* in Germany at this time, making up slightly over one per cent of the population (although Nazi guesses put it at just over double this figure).

In 1936, with the eyes of the world on Berlin during the Olympics, anti-Semitic polices were toned down. Foreign opinion during peacetime was very important to Hitler at this time, a factor which disappeared from the equation during war-time. Many Jews felt that perhaps the worst was over and things might revert to normal.

Radicalisation and physical degradation, 1938–9

Anti-Semitic policies soon shifted into a far more radical phase, however, with the marginalisation of conservative elites from late 1937 and the Nazification of foreign policy. The *Anschluss* of Austria in spring 1938 added a further 190,000 Jews, who found themselves at the receiving end of far more brutal treatment than German Jews had experienced; and in the expanded Reich, all Jews were now subjected to new measures of discrimination.

Passports were called in. New identification papers were marked with the letter 'J' for '*Jude*' (Jew), as well as new middle names Israel for males, Sarah for females – to indicate Jewish identity. The Aryanisation of Jewish property – confiscation of Jewish possessions, shops and businesses – was dramatically accelerated, and Jews were reduced to an increasingly insecure existence. By the end of the year Jews were no longer able to practise law and medicine; Jewish children were excluded from German schools; Jews were banned from concert halls, museums, swimming pools, theatres, cinemas, walking in certain areas or sitting on park benches which had not been specially designated to them.

Josef Mengele (1911–1979?)
A committed Nazi and member of the Waffen-SS, Josef Mengele attained notoriety following his appointment in 1943 as chief doctor at Auschwitz. Mengele had the power to choose who was to go straight to the gas chambers; who might first still be useful as slave labour; and who might serve his own gruesome purposes of experimentation. From 1934 he held a research post at the Institute of Hereditary Biology and Race Hygiene, specialising in the study of twins and race. After the defeat of the Third Reich, Mengele escaped to South America, where he evaded all attempts to track him down. A body found in 1985 is thought to have been that of Mengele, who may have drowned in 1979.

On 9 November 1938 (coincidentally the anniversary of the Beer Hall Putsch) Ernst vom Rath, who worked in the German Embassy in Paris, died as a result of an attack by a young Polish Jew called Herschel Grynszpan two days earlier. This was used as a pretext to unleash an orgy of violence against Jews, which Hitler discussed with Goebbels. Goebbels then coordinated the operation while Hitler distanced himself in public from what was represented as the people's 'spontaneous' revenge. Arson attacks on synagogues and looting of Jewish-owned department stores accompanied physical attacks on Jews in the *Kristallnacht* ('night of crystal') named after the heaps of broken glass from smashed windows. Official figures suggested that 91 Jews were killed; many more died during arrest and incarceration and hundreds committed suicide; 267 synagogues were destroyed and 7500 businesses vandalised. Jews were ordered to pay for the wanton destruction, while the proceeds of their insurance claims were confiscated by the state. Ordinary members of the public appear to have been shocked by the violence and destruction of property.

Despite Hitler's Reichstag 'prophecy' a few weeks later, there is little evidence that a coherent policy of mass murder was on the programme at this time. In a discussion at a meeting shortly after *Kristallnacht*, Goering, Goebbels and Heydrich squabbled and failed to agree on whether Jews should be forced to wear some form of identification, whether they should have to use separate compartments in trains, and whether they should be constrained to live in separate quarters – or encouraged to emigrate.

Emigration was in fact being actively encouraged, most energetically by Eichmann's office in Vienna. Although, having been made destitute by Nazi policies, few Jews could find ways of meeting the financial costs and paying the 'emigration tax'. In the Evian conference convened by US President Roosevelt in July 1938, it also became clear that while other countries were willing to express their sympathy, few were willing to accept unlimited numbers of Jews. It was thus becoming impossible for Jews to to continue to live within Germany; but it was also becoming increasingly impossible for them to leave.

The search for 'solutions', 1939–41

With the outbreak of the Second World War, the situation changed. With killing going on all around, and the country in a state of war, there was a brutalisation of mentalities and a lower threshold of inhibitions to be crossed. Public opinion also mattered far less, at a time when the 'problem' appeared far greater. With the absorption of parts of Czechoslovakia in 1938–9, another 118 000 Jews had come under German jurisdiction; but the number of Polish Jews was on an altogether larger scale – nearly two million (of the more than three million Polish Jews) lived in the area occupied by Germany. Many of the *Ostjuden* ('Eastern Jews') were not at all like the assimilated or integrated Jews of Germany, but were highly distinctive in customs, dress and habits.

While mass killings of Jews did take place following the invasion of Poland, organised murder was not directed primarily against Jews: the educated Polish and political elites were the major targets. In Germany itself, the principal targets of the racial state at this time were the mentally ill and 'hereditarily diseased', who became victims of the euthanasia programme. This was authorised explicitly by Hitler in a written order of October 1939 and backdated to the outbreak of the war at the start of September; notably, it officially came to a halt in August 1941 as a result of popular protest in Germany.

By contrast, there was at this time an active search for alternative 'solutions' to the Jewish Question. The main focus was on the possibility of 'resettlement', with detailed plans for a Jewish reservation around Lublin, in Poland. Following the defeat of France in May 1940, plans were also actively considered for a Jewish reservation on the island of Madagascar, off the coast of Africa, although this foundered with the German failure to defeat Britain rapidly.

Meanwhile, Polish Jews were being herded into ever more crowded ghettoes. Starvation, illness and consequent high mortality rates served merely to exacerbate the Nazis' self-imposed 'problem', in which the Nazi metaphor of Jews as a germ or source

of disease became an all-too ghastly reality. The search for 'solu
tions' was accompanied by rising frustration among those charge
with dealing with the Jewish problem. This new climate brough
about an even more radical shift.

The transition to mass extermination, 1941–2

The period following the invasion of the Soviet Union was crucial i
the transition from a search for a variety of 'solutions' to the Fina
Solution in the form of mass murder. With the decision to launc
'Operation Barbarossa' and invade the long-term ideological enem
the war entered a qualitatively new phase. This was not merely to b
a military campaign, but also a racial and political war against 'Jewis
Bolsheviks' and so-called inferior peoples. The conventional rules c
warfare were abandoned. Definitive evidence such as a written 'Hitle
order' unleashing the Final Solution is unlikely ever to be found,
indeed such a directive ever existed – which seems unlikely, give
Hitler's awareness of the sensitivity of the issue and his experienc
with the euthanasia programme. On the basis of current knowledg
a number of different interpretations can be constructed, all relyin
to some extent on speculation and surmise.

According to the Commissary Order of June 1941, anyon
considered to be even a potential enemy was to be killed outrigh
thus civilians could be summarily shot as potential Bolsheviks an
subversives. Close behind the invading army came the speci
killing squads, or *Einsatzgruppen*, who had already committe
atrocities in late June in Kovno, Bialystok, Lvov, and elsewher
Contrary to the long-held myth of the honourable German Army,
is now clear that the Army also provided invaluable logistical an
practical support to the work of the killing squads, and in som
cases actively assisted them in their murderous tasks. Within week
the target had broadened: Jewish women and children as well a
potential military opponents of the Nazis were being killed. On 3
July, Heydrich received a directive from Goering ordering him t
prepare a 'Final Solution for the Jewish question in Europe
although the character of this directive is ambiguous – it speak
explicitly of 'emigration or evacuation' as the 'solutions' to b
considered – and hence its interpretation is the subject of consider
able debate. Christopher Browning argues however that Hitle
probably first mooted a decision in favour of mass murder in Jul
1941, which was then firmed up in the autumn of 1941.

In August 1941, there was a rapid escalation of the number
involved in killing, and in the numbers murdered in mass shooting

Members of an *Einsatzgruppe* killing Polish prisoners, 1941.

(for example, at Riga); and both Eichmann and Himmler came to witness killings. Ian Kershaw points out that the notable variations in the numbers killed by different *Einsatzgruppen* suggest a considerable degree of leeway for local initiatives to be taken by different killing squads. He also argues that the fact that reinforcements had to be sent in suggests that the scale of the killing had neither been anticipated nor planned for in advance.

Mass murder had now begun, and a crucial threshold had been crossed. The invasion of Russia had also again dramatically increased the numbers of Jews under German domination, and hence the scale of the 'problem'.

Experience soon showed that shooting people into mass graves was less than efficient. It was relatively public and witnesses reported back what they had seen. It was also difficult to gain the compliance of those having to shoot naked women and children in cold blood, unless they had first been plied with copious quantities of alcohol. Experts from the now terminated euthanasia or 'T4' programme were brought in to give their advice. On 3 September, **Zyklon B gas** was first tested on Soviet prisoners held at Auschwitz.

Philippe Burrin dates the decision to engage in the systematic mass murder of European Jews to the early autumn. The decision that Jews should be deported from the German Reich and the Protectorate of Bohemia and Moravia to the East was taken in mid-September, following the decision a month earlier that German Jews should be forced to wear the Jewish badge from September onwards. In October, emigration – which had in any event been very

Zyklon B gas: a highly poisonous gas used in the gas chambers of extermination camps such as Auschwitz. Other methods of killing, such as shooting people into mass graves, or gassing with carbon monoxide exhaust fumes in vans which had been specially designed for this purpose, were found to be less 'efficient'.

difficult – was completely prohibited. But it was not clear where Jews would be 'resettled', given problems with the Russian campaign. Already overcrowded ghettos, such as that in Lódz, began to receive ever larger numbers. Death rates from disease and starvation continued to rise, and the notion of selecting weaker Jews to be disposed of quickly no longer seemed so outrageous. On December the first mass killing took place at Chelmno. Those selected from the Lódz ghetto were gassed to death.

Christian Gerlach claims the turning point was only reached in early December 1941. He distinguishes between the killings of Soviet and other Jews within the occupied territories, and the decision to deport Jews from across Europe. It was only as the war turned into a *world* war with the Japanese attack on Pearl Harbor and Germany's declaration of war on the USA, that Hitler took the ultimate decision to turn his 'prophecy' of January 1939 into murderous reality. On 12 December 1941, Hitler announced to party leaders that the Final Solution now meant genocide.

The meeting at the lakeside villa near Berlin in January 1942, known as the Wannsee conference, had originally been scheduled for early December and then postponed. It initially grew out of Heydrich's directive from Goering of the previous summer to draw a programme for the final solution, and also revisited the question of the definition of *Mischlinge*. Separate initiatives were now

Female prisoners in barracks at Auschwitz, 1945.

coordinated, and the Final Solution as a programme of mass murder moved into an altogether more terrifying phase.

A series of extermination centres were developed (Sobibor, Treblinka, Belzec, Majdanek, as well as the notorious Auschwitz II at Birkenau). Alongside their technological refinement, the Nazis also used psychological means in their implementation of mass murder. Gas chambers were disguised as shower rooms, and posters warning of the alleged dangers of lice were instrumental in calming those walking unwittingly to their death. At this stage, very large numbers were involved in the system of extermination: bureaucrats organising the deportation of Jews or constructing the train timetables; doctors involved in 'medical' experiments and 'selections'; industrialists benefiting from slave labour; technocrats dealing with population policy; SS thugs at the sadistic front line, as well as those prisoners forced to assist them. Although there were isolated uprisings, as in Warsaw, affected Jewish communities, facing almost certain defeat in face of intolerable odds, often resorted to traditions of 'anticipatory compliance' and attempts at 'alleviation'. As Raul Hilberg points out, these methods had worked tolerably well for centuries; but which, in the face of this unprecedented evil, were now met by unprecedented disaster.

Every reconstruction of these events relies to a large extent on piecing together different fragments of evidence in the light of wider knowledge of Hitler's psychology, and that of those around him, with alternative interpretations possible for many ambiguous sources. It is also notable that all the historians mentioned here to a greater or lesser extent abandon the simple dichotomy between intentionalist and functionalist explanations. They focus rather on the constant interaction between Hitler's radical ideological goals (and fluctuating moods), on the one hand, and the wider field of forces and changing pressures in which he operated, on the other. Constant improvisation in the face of mounting problems and a narrowing of possible alternative 'solutions' provides little evidence of careful prior planning with only one possible 'programme' in mind; yet, varied initiatives did not suddenly come out of the blue, but were constantly given sanction, impetus and direction from the highest level.

To what extent were 'ordinary Germans' responsible for the Holocaust?

Immediately after the war was over, the Americans – briefly – held a notion of 'collective guilt', assuming that all Germans were bad

Germans. At the same time, many Germans professed that they ha 'known nothing about it', and that the post-war revelations of th atrocities 'committed in their name' came as a terrible shoc Neither of these positions is an accurate representation.

A nation of perpetrators?

Considerable controversy was occasioned by the publication in 199 of Daniel Jonah Goldhagen's thesis, *Hitler's Willing Executioner Ordinary Germans and the Holocaust,* which resurrected th notion of collective guilt. Making a strong distinction betwee 'Germans' and 'Jews', Goldhagen suggests that the explanatic of the Holocaust is basically very simple: Germans killed Jev because they wanted to kill Jews. German political culture wa deeply flawed by a long-standing and peculiarly virulent form 'eliminationist anti-Semitism'.

There are all manner of theoretical, methodological ar historical flaws in this highly emotive and persuasively writte text. Goldhagen generalises, citing a small sample of peop drawn from a cross-section of German society as 'all Germans He fails to explore the ways in which these 'ordinary men' – als studied by Christopher Browning, with rather different conclu sions – might have been radicalised under conditions of extrem brutality and warfare. The work fails to compare them wit similar perpetrators from other nationalities, such Ukrainians, Romanians, and collaborators from the Balt states. It reifies the 'collective mentality' of 'eliminationist ant Semitism', suggesting that it somehow hibernated acro decades of the eighteenth century when it remained 'laten rather than empirically visible in the historical record. Th highly 'culturalist' explanation in terms of a collective mentali allegedly persisting across centuries is suddenly abandoned i favour of an institutional explanation; after 1945, with the intro duction of democratic political structures, Germans apparent suddenly ceased to have this anti-Semitic mentality.

It could in contrast be argued that 'ordinary Germans' we in fact radicalised by the conditions of warfare. The situation. explanation suggests that ordinary people of any backgrour can be driven to commit otherwise unthinkable atrocities und extraordinary circumstances. The 'ordinary men' of polic battalions and those drafted to the front were not th ideologically committed anti-Semites of the SS units or th killing squads. It also seems, from the work of Omer Bartov, tha

Rudolf Vrba (b. 1925)
Born in Slovakia, Vrba was deported to Auschwitz in 1942. Vrba and a fellow inmate, Wetzler, miraculously succeeded in escaping in April 1944, and produced the *Vrba-Wetzler Report* with detailed information on the Holocaust. Through reports such as this and from other survivors, and news and rumour from soldiers, engineers, and other eye-witnesses at the front, the fact that 'resettlement' actually meant organised murder was widespread knowledge both among foreign governments and within Nazi Germany itself. But reports of such unthinkable atrocities were widely met with sheer disbelief. One of the minority of lucky survivors, after the war Vrba emigrated first to Israel, and subsequently to Canada, where he became a university professor.

'ordinary Germans' had been to some degree affected by Nazi indoctrination and the pervasive ideology of anti-Semitism to which they had been exposed in preceding years. This difference between their attitudes and those of fellow killers from other backgrounds was the product of recent socialisation, not evidence of a centuries-old difference in 'collective mentality'.

Violence, legality and apathy

Saul Friedländer characterises Hitler's brand of anti-Semitism as one of 'redemptive anti-Semitism': a 'synthesis of a murderous rage and an "idealistic" goal', namely the total eradication of the Jewish race. This was common among members of the party elite, in the SS and SD, and among party radicals, but was not shared by the wider population, where 'anti-Jewish attitudes were more in the realm of tacit acquiescence or varying degrees of compliance'. (Saul Friedländer, *Nazi Germany and the Jews: Vol. 1: The Years of Persecution, 1933–39*, HarperCollins, 1997, pp. 3–4.)

During the 1930s, popular attitudes covered a wide spectrum. Hitler himself was well aware of this when he toned down his own virulent anti-Semitism in electoral campaigns before 1933. Once in power, while party radicals repeatedly demanded more violent actions, Hitler was unwilling to jeopardise his personal popularity and he called off the Jewish boycott of April 1933. He also reverted to legal measures in the Nuremberg Laws and he distanced himself from the *Kristallnacht* of 1938. The party radicals who engaged with glee on the rampages of looting, beating up and murdering of Jews were a small minority. Their criminal actions were both unleashed and sanctioned by the Nazi government, but many other Germans reacted with shame and horror to these events.

Primo Levi (1919–87) born in Turin, Italy, Levi was trained as a chemist. A member of the anti-Fascist resistance in Italy, he was arrested and deported to Auschwitz in 1944. He wrote numerous books and poetry after the war, including *If this is a Man* and *The Periodic Table*. Unable finally to live with the guilt and pain of survival, he committed suicide in 1987.

Germans had generally fewer scruples about the legalisation of discrimination. Jews could thus be stigmatised, removed from their status as German citizens with equal rights in German society, and ultimately removed from living in Germany and indeed from life itself, with only minimal protest on the part of bystanders and onlookers. News leaking out about the Holocaust was reacted to with apathy and disbelief. This stood in stark contrast to the public outcry supported by the Catholic Bishop von Galen against the euthanasia programme. Had a similar outcry been unleashed against the systematic vilification, violent maltreatment and sporadic killing of German Jews in the 1930s, the fate of European Jews might have been very different.

Kershaw points out that the persecution of the Jews 'would n have been possible without the apathy and widespread indifferen which was the common response to the propaganda of hate'. would also not have been possible 'without the silence of chur hierarchies ... and without the consent ranging to active complici of other prominent sections of the German elites – the civil servi bureaucracy, the armed forces, and not least leading sectors industry' (Ian Kershaw, *Popular Opinion*, p. 372).

Hitler's own ideological goals and obsessive character we clearly central to the dynamics of the Holocaust. However, Hitler views could only have had the impact they did within the extraord nary, quasi-feudal system of power, repression, hatred ar aggression that had been constructed over the space of a very fe years. This system had the active consent or compliance of the ke elites, while the vast majority of 'ordinary Germans' retreated in their private spheres, primarily concerned with personal surviv and matters of self-interest.

There can be no single or simple explanation for the Holocaus neither Hitler's intentions, nor the curious structures of power, ne the alleged character of Germany's collective mentalities, can stand easy scapegoats for this virtually incomprehensible crime.

The Holocaust: How did Nazi racial policies turn into genocide?

1. Read the following extract and answer the question.

   *'Europe cannot find peace until the Jewish question has been solved ...
   Today I will once more be a prophet: if the international Jewish
   financiers in and outside Europe should succeed in plunging the
   nations once more into a world war, then the result will not be the
   Bolshevising of the earth, and thus the victory of Jewry, but the
   annihilation of the Jewish race in Europe!'*

   (Hitler's speech to the Reichstag, 30 January 1939, reprinted in Jeremy
   Noakes and Geoffrey Pridham (eds), *Nazism: Foreign Policy, War and
   Racial Extermination*, vol. 3, Exeter: Exeter Studies in History 1988,
   p. 1049.)

   How useful is this source in understanding the transition of Nazi racial
   policies into genocide?

2. In what ways, if at all, should 'ordinary Germans' be held responsible for
   the Holocaust?

itler: an assessment

Hitler, popular opinion and opposition

- Hitler's popularity was based on the 'Hitler myth': the image of Hitler as a national saviour, representing and leading the people to a glorious common future.
- The rapidly growing apparatus of terror was targeted selectively at political opponents and 'racial' victims of the regime, who were identified and vilified in propaganda.
- Key elites in the civil service, the economy and the Army went along with the regime until it was too late.
- Isolated acts of opposition by a minority were readily suppressed.

Hitler, foreign policy and war

- Following the First World War (1914–18), the 1919 Treaty of Versailles created new sources of tension and conflict. The international system was highly unstable.
- Many Germans shared the view that the Treaty of Versailles should be revised; some nationalists also harboured wider aims for German domination of central Europe.
- Hitler had far more ambitious plans for European expansion and ultimately planned on world domination. He also seized and exploited opportunities as they arose.
- Hitler abandoned conventional economic policies in order to combine rapid rearmament with consumer satisfaction, aiming for a quick war of 'lightning strikes' and exploitation of conquered territories.
- Hitler played a major role in turning the war into one of unprecedented ideological and racial aggression, and turning European conflict into world war.

Hitler and the Holocaust

- Hitler's rabid anti-Semitism set the general tone and overall direction of racial policy. In the context of pressures from party radicals, Hitler also kept an eye on the views of civil servants and national conservatives, and on domestic and foreign opinion.
- Racial policy developed through a series of stages, in which there were struggles between those advocating brutality and violence and those proposing the generally more acceptable 'legalisation' of further discrimination.
- Constant improvisation included policies of impoverishment, exclusion, emigration and 'resettlement' as potential 'solutions' to the 'Jewish question', while the disabled and mentally ill victims of the 'euthanasia' campaign, and the Polish intelligentsia and political elites, were the first targets of organised policies of mass murder.
- While Hitler's 'intentions' were undoubtedly central, the 'Final Solution' which emerged in 1941 seems to have been more a result of improvisation in conditions of growing brutality and chaos than the unleashing of a preconceived plan or 'programme'.

Further reading

Texts specifically designed for students

Overy, R. J., *The Origins of the Second World War* (Harlow: Pearson, 2nd edn., 1998)

Norbert, F., *National Socialist Rule in Germany: The Führer State, 1933–1945* (Oxford: Blackwell 1993; original German 1987)

Kershaw, I., *The Nazi Dictatorship: Problems and Perspectives of Interpretation* (Arnold, 4th edn, 2000)

Texts for more advanced study

Bartov, O. (ed.), *The Holocaust: Origins, Implementation, Aftermath* (Routledge, 2000) contains key articles.

Bell, P. M. H., *The Second World War in Europe* (Longman, 2nd edn., 1997) is a clear guide through the major developments in the light of historical debates.

Gellately, R., *Backing Hitler. Coercion and Consent in the Third Reich* (Oxford, 2001)

Hildebrand, K., *The Third Reich* (London: George Allen and Unwin, 1984; original German 1979) is an overview from an 'intentionalist' or 'Hitler-centric' perspective.

Kershaw, I., *Hitler 1889–1936: Hubris* (Penguin, 1998) and *Hitler 1936–1945: Nemesis* (Penguin, 2000) are currently the definitive biography of Hitler; see also *The 'Hitler Myth': Image and Reality in the Third Reich* (Oxford University Press, 1987) and *Popular Opinion and Political Dissent in the Third Reich* (Clarendon Press, 1983) both of which are crucial for understanding popular support, nonconformity and dissent.

Martel, G. (ed.), *The Origins of the Second World War Reconsidered* (Routledge, 2nd edn., 1999) contains key articles summarising current critiques of the Taylor thesis.

Noakes, J. and Pridham, G. (eds), *Nazism* (Exeter: Exeter Studies in History, 1983–1998), four volumes: 'The Rise to Power, 1919–1934' (vol. 1); 'State, Economy and Society, 1933–1939' (vol. 2); 'Foreign Policy, War and Racial Extermination' (vol. 3) and 'The German Home Front in World War II' (vol. 4).

Taylor, A. J. P., *The Origins of the Second World War* (Hamish Hamilton, 1961) is a highly controversial classic.

Welch, D., *The Third Reich. Politics and Propaganda* (Routledge, 2nd edn., 2002)

ᵭdex